I0788871

GOD'S ANGELS

What the Bible Has to Say

GOD'S ANGELS

What the Bible Has to Say

Compiled by Eugene Carvalho

God's Angels: What the Bible Has to Say

Copyright © 2019 by Eugene Carvalho

ISBN: 9781798885574

Printed in the United States of America

All rights reserved, without written permission from the publisher, except as provided by United States copyright laws.

"Scripture taken from the
NEW AMERICAN STANDARD BIBLE ®
Copyright ©
1960,1962,1963,1968,1971,1972,1973,1975,1977,1995
by The Lockman Foundation. Used by permission."

Scripture quotations from The Authorized (King James) Version. Rights in the Authorized Version in the United Kingdom are vested in the Crown. Reproduced by permission of the Crown's patentee, Cambridge University Press

*To the Body of Christ.
May this compilation bless you richly!
With love…*

TABLE OF CONTENTS

PURPOSE AND ACKNOWLEDGEMENTS

The infallible Word of God for faith and conduct informs us that the Holy Spirit gives gifts to men and women of the Body of Christ. It states: "the gifts edify the body for the building up of the saints" (Eph. 4:12). I hope the talents and gifts the Lord has given me will be a blessing to someone else through the reading of this compilation.

I am grateful for the love from all family members, especially my wife Mercedes Carvalho. I am also grateful for the knowledge, wisdom and love of many pastors, teachers, and saints that the Lord has used to bless me. Lastly, I must not forget a special thank you to my friend Kathryn Regan for proofreading this material.

GOD'S ANGELS

Let's turn to the book of Hebrews for some insight. The Bible says, "God, after He spoke long ago to the fathers in the prophets in many portions and in many ways, in these last days has spoken to us in His Son, whom He appointed heir of all things, through whom also He made the world" (Heb. 1:1-2).[1] Those scriptures inform me Jesus made everything and owns everything. The following verse tells me the same. "For by Him all things were created, both in the heavens and on earth, visible and invisible, whether thrones or dominions or rulers or authorities—all things have been created through Him and for Him" (Col. 1:16).

Some facts regarding the angels that Jesus created include: they are ministering spirits sent out to serve, they encamp around those who fear Him, there's joy before the angels over one sinner, they shut the mouths of lions, and they opened the prison doors. This compilation investigates every scripture from Genesis to Revelation that discusses God's angels.

Angels are very powerful. The Bible tells us that Sennacherib king of Assyria came against King Hezekiah, however, the Lord informed Hezekiah that he would not come to the city or shoot an arrow there. The Bible records, "And it came to pass that night, that the angel of the Lord went out, and smote in the camp of the Assyrians an hundred fourscore and five thousand: and when they arose early in the morning, behold, they were all dead corpses" (2 Kings 19:35). Wow, we see in that verse the Lord sent one angel and when that angel was finished flapping his winds

---

[1] All Scripture quotations, unless otherwise noted, are from the *New American Standard Bible.*

around there was 185,000 dead corpses. Now that's one powerful military. One angel took care of 185,000 problems in one night. You might have a lot of problems but I don't think you have 185,000 of them. Therefore, one angel could take care of all your problems over night.

When Judas, the chief priests, the officers of the temple, and the elders came against Jesus, He made a powerful statement. Jesus stated twelve legions of angels are available in the Kingdom of God if someone is in trouble. (see Matt. 26:53). I was informed there are 6000 angels in a legion, so twelve legions would be 72,000 angels available to His servants if need be. Now if one angel can kill 185,000 in one night can you imagine what 72,000 angels could do?

My favorite scriptures regarding angels are, "And I beheld, and I heard the voice of many angels round about the throne and the beasts and the elders: and the number of them was ten thousand times ten thousand, and thousands of thousands; Saying with a loud voice, Worthy is the Lamb that was slain to receive power, and riches, and wisdom, and strength, and honour, and glory, and blessing" (Rev. 5:11-12 KJV). With that said, lets' go to the infallible scriptures that discuss God's angels.

ANGEL IN THE OLD TESTAMENT

The Angel Told Her, "Return to Your Mistress."

"Now the angel of the Lord found her by a spring of water in the wilderness, by the spring on the way to Shur. He said, 'Hagar, Sarai's maid, where have you come from and where are you going?' And she said, 'I am fleeing from the presence of my mistress Sarai.' Then the angel of the Lord said to her, 'Return to your mistress, and submit yourself to her authority.' Moreover, the angel of the Lord said to her, 'I will greatly multiply your descendants so that they will be too many to count.' The angel of the Lord said to her further, 'Behold, you are with child, And you will bear a son; And you shall call his name Ishmael, Because the Lord has given heed to your affliction. He will be a wild donkey of a man, His hand will be against everyone, And everyone's hand will be against him; And he will live to the east of all his brothers.' Then she called the name of the Lord who spoke to her, 'You are a God who sees"; for she said, 'Have I even remained alive here after seeing Him?' Therefore the well was called Beer-lahai-roi; behold, it is between Kadesh and Bered" (Ge. 16:7-14).

The Angel of God Called to Hagar from Heaven

"When the water in the skin was used up, she left the boy under one of the bushes. Then she went and sat down opposite him, about a bowshot away, for she said, 'Do not let me see the boy die.' And she sat opposite him, and lifted up her voice and wept. God heard the lad crying; and the angel of God called to Hagar from heaven and said to her, 'What is the matter with you, Hagar? Do not fear, for God has heard the voice of the lad where he is. Arise, lift up the lad, and hold him by the hand, for I will make a great nation of him.' Then God opened her eyes and she saw a well of water; and she went and filled the skin with water and gave the lad a drink" (Ge. 21:15-19).

The Angel Called to Abraham a Second Time

"Then they came to the place of which God had told him; and Abraham built the altar there and arranged the wood, and bound his son Isaac and laid him on the altar, on top of the wood. Abraham stretched out his hand and took the knife to slay his son. But the angel of the Lord called to him from heaven and said, 'Abraham, Abraham!' And he said, 'Here I am.' He said, 'Do not stretch out your hand against the lad, and do nothing to him; for now I know that you fear God, since you have not withheld your son, your only son, from Me.' Then Abraham raised his eyes and looked, and behold, behind him a ram caught in the thicket by his horns; and Abraham went and took the ram and offered him up for a burnt offering in the place of his son. Abraham called the name of that place The Lord Will Provide, as it is said to this day, 'In the mount of the Lord it will be provided.' Then the angel of the Lord called to Abraham a second time from heaven, and said, 'By Myself I have sworn, declares the Lord, because you have done this thing and have not withheld your son, your only son, indeed I will greatly bless you, and I will greatly multiply your seed as the stars of the heavens and as the sand which is on the seashore; and your seed shall possess the gate of their enemies. In your seed all the nations of the earth shall be blessed, because you have obeyed My voice.' So Abraham returned to his young men, and they arose and went together to Beersheba; and Abraham lived at Beersheba" (Ge. 22:9-19).

He Will Send His Angel Before You

"Now Abraham was old, advanced in age; and the Lord had blessed Abraham in every way. Abraham said to his servant, the oldest of his household, who had charge of all that he owned, 'Please place your hand under my thigh, and I will make you swear by the Lord, the God of heaven and the God of earth, that you shall not take a wife for my son from the daughters of the Canaanites, among whom I live, but you will go to my country and to my relatives, and take a wife for my son Isaac.' The servant said to him, 'Suppose the woman is not willing to follow me to this land; should I take your son back to the land from where you came?' Then Abraham said to him, 'Beware that you do not take my son back there! The Lord, the God of heaven, who took me from my father's house and from the land of my birth, and who spoke to me and who swore to me, saying, "To your descendants I will give this land," He will send His angel before you, and you will take a wife for my son from there. But if the woman is not willing to follow you, then you will be free from this my oath; only do not take my son back there.' So the servant placed his hand under the thigh of Abraham his master, and swore to him concerning this matter" (Ge. 24:1-9).

Chapter Two

His Angel Will Make Your Journey Successful

"Then the girl ran and told her mother's household about these things. Now Rebekah had a brother whose name was Laban; and Laban ran outside to the man at the spring. When he saw the ring and the bracelets on his sister's wrists, and when he heard the words of Rebekah his sister, saying, 'This is what the man said to me,' he went to the man; and behold, he was standing by the camels at the spring. And he said, 'Come in, blessed of the Lord! Why do you stand outside since I have prepared the house, and a place for the camels?' So the man entered the house. Then Laban unloaded the camels, and he gave straw and feed to the camels, and water to wash his feet and the feet of the men who were with him. But when food was set before him to eat, he said, 'I will not eat until I have told my business.' And he said, 'Speak on.' So he said, 'I am Abraham's servant. The Lord has greatly blessed my master, so that he has become rich; and He has given him flocks and herds, and silver and gold, and servants and maids, and camels and donkeys. Now Sarah my master's wife bore a son to my master in her old age, and he has given him all that he has. My master made me swear, saying, 'You shall not take a wife for my son from the daughters of the Canaanites, in whose land I live; but you shall go to my father's house and to my relatives, and take a wife for my son.' I said to my master, 'Suppose the woman does not follow me.' He said to me, 'The Lord, before whom I have walked, will send His angel with you to make your journey successful, and you will take a wife for my son from my relatives and from my father's house; then you will be free from my oath, when you come to my relatives; and if they do not give her to you, you will be free from my oath'" (Ge. 24:28-41).

The Angel Talked to Jacob in a Dream

"Now Jacob heard the words of Laban's sons, saying, 'Jacob has taken away all that was our father's, and from what belonged to our father he has made all this wealth.' Jacob saw the attitude of Laban, and behold, it was not friendly toward him as formerly. Then the Lord said to Jacob, 'Return to the land of your fathers and to your relatives, and I will be with you.' So Jacob sent and called Rachel and Leah to his flock in the field, and said to them, 'I see your father's attitude, that it is not friendly toward me as formerly, but the God of my father has been with me. You know that I have served your father with all my strength. Yet your father has cheated me and changed my wages ten times; however, God did not allow him to hurt me. If he spoke thus, "The speckled shall be your wages," then all the flock brought forth speckled; and if he spoke thus, "The striped shall be your wages," then all the flock brought forth striped. Thus God has taken away your father's livestock and given them to me. And it came about at the time when the flock were mating that I lifted up my eyes and saw in a dream, and behold, the male goats which were mating were striped, speckled, and mottled. Then the angel of God said to me in the dream, "Jacob," and I said, "Here I am." He said, "Lift up now your eyes and see that all the male goats which are mating are striped, speckled, and mottled; for I have seen all that Laban has been doing to you. I am the God of Bethel, where you anointed a pillar, where you made a vow to Me; now arise, leave this land, and return to the land of your birth.'" Rachel and Leah said to him, 'Do we still have any portion or inheritance in our father's house? Are we not reckoned by him as foreigners? For he has sold us, and has also entirely consumed our purchase price. Surely all the wealth which God has taken away from our father belongs to us and our children; now then, do whatever God has said to you'" (Ge. 31:1-16).

The Angel Redeemed Me from All Evil

"When Israel saw Joseph's sons, he said, 'Who are these?' Joseph said to his father, 'They are my sons, whom God has given me here.' So he said, 'Bring them to me, please, that I may bless them.' Now the eyes of Israel were so dim from age that he could not see. Then Joseph brought them close to him, and he kissed them and embraced them. Israel said to Joseph, 'I never expected to see your face, and behold, God has let me see your children as well.' Then Joseph took them from his knees, and bowed with his face to the ground. Joseph took them both, Ephraim with his right hand toward Israel's left, and Manasseh with his left hand toward Israel's right, and brought them close to him. But Israel stretched out his right hand and laid it on the head of Ephraim, who was the younger, and his left hand on Manasseh's head, crossing his hands, although Manasseh was the firstborn. He blessed Joseph, and said, 'The God before whom my fathers Abraham and Isaac walked, The God who has been my shepherd all my life to this day, The angel who has redeemed me from all evil, Bless the lads; And may my name live on in them, And the names of my fathers Abraham and Isaac; And may they grow into a multitude in the midst of the earth'" (Ge. 48:8-16).

The Angel Appeared to Him in a Blazing Fire from the Midst of a Bush

"Now Moses was pasturing the flock of Jethro his father-in-law, the priest of Midian; and he led the flock to the west side of the wilderness and came to Horeb, the mountain of God. The angel of the Lord appeared to him in a blazing fire from the midst of a bush; and he looked, and behold, the bush was burning with fire, yet the bush was not consumed. So Moses said, 'I must turn aside now and see this marvelous sight, why the bush is not burned up.' When the Lord saw that he turned aside to look, God called to him from the midst of the bush and said, 'Moses, Moses!' And he said, 'Here I am.' Then He said, 'Do not come near here; remove your sandals from your feet, for the place on which you are standing is holy ground.' He said also, 'I am the God of your father, the God of Abraham, the God of Isaac, and the God of Jacob.' Then Moses hid his face, for he was afraid to look at God" (Ex. 3:1-6).

The Angel Went Before the Camp

"The angel of God, who had been going before the camp of Israel, moved and went behind them; and the pillar of cloud moved from before them and stood behind them. So it came between the camp of Egypt and the camp of Israel; and there was the cloud along with the darkness, yet it gave light at night. Thus the one did not come near the other all night" (Ex. 14:19-20

Chapter Two

I Will Send an Angel Before You to Guard You

"Behold, I am going to send an angel before you to guard you along the way and to bring you into the place which I have prepared. Be on your guard before him and obey his voice; do not be rebellious toward him, for he will not pardon your transgression, since My name is in him. But if you truly obey his voice and do all that I say, then I will be an enemy to your enemies and an adversary to your adversaries. For My angel will go before you and bring you in to the land of the Amorites, the Hittites, the Perizzites, the Canaanites, the Hivites and the Jebusites; and I will completely destroy them. You shall not worship their gods, nor serve them, nor do according to their deeds; but you shall utterly overthrow them and break their sacred pillars in pieces. But you shall serve the Lord your God, and He will bless your bread and your water; and I will remove sickness from your midst. There shall be no one miscarrying or barren in your land; I will fulfill the number of your days. I will send My terror ahead of you, and throw into confusion all the people among whom you come, and I will make all your enemies turn their backs to you. I will send hornets ahead of you so that they will drive out the Hivites, the Canaanites, and the Hittites before you. I will not drive them out before you in a single year, that the land may not become desolate and the beasts of the field become too numerous for you. I will drive them out before you little by little, until you become fruitful and take possession of the land. I will fix your boundary from the Red Sea to the sea of the Philistines, and from the wilderness to the River Euphrates; for I will deliver the inhabitants of the land into your hand, and you will drive them out before you. You shall make no covenant with them or with their gods. They shall not live in your land, because they will make you sin against Me; for if you serve their gods, it will surely be a snare to you" (Ex. 23:20-33).

My Angel Shall Go Before You

"On the next day Moses said to the people, 'You yourselves have committed a great sin; and now I am going up to the Lord, perhaps I can make atonement for your sin.' Then Moses returned to the Lord, and said, 'Alas, this people has committed a great sin, and they have made a god of gold for themselves. But now, if You will, forgive their sin—and if not, please blot me out from Your book which You have written!' The Lord said to Moses, 'Whoever has sinned against Me, I will blot him out of My book. But go now, lead the people where I told you. Behold, My angel shall go before you; nevertheless in the day when I punish, I will punish them for their sin.' Then the Lord smote the people, because of what they did with the calf which Aaron had made" (Ex. 32:30-35).

An Angel Will Drive Them Out

"Then the Lord spoke to Moses, 'Depart, go up from here, you and the people whom you have brought up from the land of Egypt, to the land of which I swore to Abraham, Isaac, and Jacob, saying, "To your descendants I will give it." I will send an angel before you and I will drive out the Canaanite, the Amorite, the Hittite, the Perizzite, the Hivite and the Jebusite. Go up to a land flowing with milk and honey; for I will not go up in your midst, because you are an obstinate people, and I might destroy you on the way'" (Ex. 33:1-3).

An Angel Brought Us out of Egypt

"From Kadesh Moses then sent messengers to the king of Edom: 'Thus your brother Israel has said, "You know all the hardship that has befallen us; that our fathers went down to Egypt, and we stayed in Egypt a long time, and the Egyptians treated us and our fathers badly. But when we cried out to the Lord, He heard our voice and sent an angel and brought us out from Egypt; now behold, we are at Kadesh, a town on the edge of your territory. Please let us pass through your land. We will not pass through field or through vineyard; we will not even drink water from a well. We will go along the king's highway, not turning to the right or left, until we pass through your territory'"" (Nu. 20:14-17).

The Angel Took His Stand

"So Balaam arose in the morning, and saddled his donkey and went with the leaders of Moab. But God was angry because he was going, and the angel of the Lord took his stand in the way as an adversary against him. Now he was riding on his donkey and his two servants were with him. When the donkey saw the angel of the Lord standing in the way with his drawn sword in his hand, the donkey turned off from the way and went into the field; but Balaam struck the donkey to turn her back into the way. Then the angel of the Lord stood in a narrow path of the vineyards, with a wall on this side and a wall on that side. When the donkey saw the angel of the Lord, she pressed herself to the wall and pressed Balaam's foot against the wall, so he struck her again. The angel of the Lord went further, and stood in a narrow place where there was no way to turn to the right hand or the left. When the donkey saw the angel of the Lord, she lay down under Balaam; so Balaam was angry and struck the donkey with his stick. And the Lord opened the mouth of the donkey, and she said to Balaam, 'What have I done to you, that you have struck me these three times?' Then Balaam said to the donkey, 'Because you have made a mockery of me! If there had been a sword in my hand, I would have killed you by now.' The donkey said to Balaam, 'Am I not your donkey on which you have ridden all your life to this day? Have I ever been accustomed to do so to you?' And he said, 'No'" (Nu. 22:21-30).

An Angel with His Drawn Sword in His Hand

"Then the Lord opened the eyes of Balaam, and he saw the angel of the Lord standing in the way with his drawn sword in his hand; and he bowed all the way to the ground. The angel of the Lord said to him, 'Why have you struck your donkey these three times? Behold, I have come out as an adversary, because your way was contrary to me. But the donkey saw me and turned aside from me these three times. If she had not turned aside from me, I would surely have killed you just now, and let her live.' Balaam said to the angel of the Lord, 'I have sinned, for I did not know that you were standing in the way against me. Now then, if it is displeasing to you, I will turn back.' But the angel of the Lord said to Balaam, 'Go with the men, but you shall speak only the word which I tell you.' So Balaam went along with the leaders of Balak" (Nu. 22:31-35).

The Angel Spoke to All the Sons of Israel

"Now the angel of the Lord came up from Gilgal to Bochim. And he said, 'I brought you up out of Egypt and led you into the land which I have sworn to your fathers; and I said, "I will never break My covenant with you, and as for you, you shall make no covenant with the inhabitants of this land; you shall tear down their altars." But you have not obeyed Me; what is this you have done? Therefore I also said, "I will not drive them out before you; but they will become as thorns in your sides and their gods will be a snare to you.'" When the angel of the Lord spoke these words to all the sons of Israel, the people lifted up their voices and wept. So they named that place Bochim; and there they sacrificed to the Lord" (Jdg. 2:1-5).

"Curse Meroz," Said the Angel

"The kings came and fought; Then fought the kings of Canaan At Taanach near the waters of Megiddo; They took no plunder in silver. The stars fought from heaven, From their courses they fought against Sisera. The torrent of Kishon swept them away, The ancient torrent, the torrent Kishon. O my soul, march on with strength. Then the horses' hoofs beat From the dashing, the dashing of his valiant steeds. 'Curse Meroz,' said the angel of the Lord, 'Utterly curse its inhabitants; Because they did not come to the help of the Lord, To the help of the Lord against the warriors'" (Jdg. 5:19-23).

The Angel Said to Gideon, "The Lord Is With You, O Valiant Warrior."

"Then the angel of the Lord came and sat under the oak that was in Ophrah, which belonged to Joash the Abiezrite as his son Gideon was beating out wheat in the wine press in order to save it from the Midianites. The angel of the Lord appeared to him and said to him, 'The Lord is with you, O valiant warrior.' Then Gideon said to him, 'O my lord, if the Lord is with us, why then has all this happened to us? And where are all His miracles which our fathers told us about, saying, "Did not the Lord bring us up from Egypt?" But now the Lord has abandoned us and given us into the hand of Midian.' The Lord looked at him and said, 'Go in this your strength and deliver Israel from the hand of Midian. Have I not sent you?' He said to Him, 'O Lord, how shall I deliver Israel? Behold, my family is the least in Manasseh, and I am the youngest in my father's house.' But the Lord said to him, 'Surely I will be with you, and you shall defeat Midian as one man.' So Gideon said to Him, 'If now I have found favor in Your sight, then show me a sign that it is You who speak with me. Please do not depart from here, until I come back to You, and bring out my offering and lay it before You.' And He said, 'I will remain until you return'" (Jdg. 6:11-18).

The Angel Spoke to Him

"Then Gideon went in and prepared a young goat and unleavened bread from an ephah of flour; he put the meat in a basket and the broth in a pot, and brought them out to him under the oak and presented them. The angel of God said to him, 'Take the meat and the unleavened bread and lay them on this rock, and pour out the broth.' And he did so. Then the angel of the Lord put out the end of the staff that was in his hand and touched the meat and the unleavened bread; and fire sprang up from the rock and consumed the meat and the unleavened bread. Then the angel of the Lord vanished from his sight. When Gideon saw that he was the angel of the Lord, he said, 'Alas, O Lord GOD! For now I have seen the angel of the LORD face to face.' The Lord said to him, 'Peace to you, do not fear; you shall not die.' Then Gideon built an altar there to the Lord and named it The Lord is Peace. To this day it is still in Ophrah of the Abiezrites" (Jdg. 6:19-24).

The Angel Told Her, "You Shall Conceive and Give Birth to a Son."

"There was a certain man of Zorah, of the family of the Danites, whose name was Manoah; and his wife was barren and had borne no children. Then the angel of the Lord appeared to the woman and said to her, 'Behold now, you are barren and have borne no children, but you shall conceive and give birth to a son. Now therefore, be careful not to drink wine or strong drink, nor eat any unclean thing. For behold, you shall conceive and give birth to a son, and no razor shall come upon his head, for the boy shall be a Nazirite to God from the womb; and he shall begin to deliver Israel from the hands of the Philistines.' Then the woman came and told her husband, saying, 'A man of God came to me and his appearance was like the appearance of the angel of God, very awesome. And I did not ask him where he came from, nor did he tell me his name.

But he said to me, "Behold, you shall conceive and give birth to a son, and now you shall not drink wine or strong drink nor eat any unclean thing, for the boy shall be a Nazirite to God from the womb to the day of his death"'" (Jdg. 13:2-7).

The Angel Came Again

"Then Manoah entreated the Lord and said, 'O Lord, please let the man of God whom You have sent come to us again that he may teach us what to do for the boy who is to be born.' God listened to the voice of Manoah; and the angel of God came again to the woman as she was sitting in the field, but Manoah her husband was not with her. So the woman ran quickly and told her husband, 'Behold, the man who came the other day has appeared to me.' Then Manoah arose and followed his wife, and when he came to the man he said to him, 'Are you the man who spoke to the woman?' And he said, 'I am.' Manoah said, 'Now when your words come to pass, what shall be the boy's mode of life and his vocation?' So the angel of the Lord said to Manoah, 'Let the woman pay attention to all that I said. She should not eat anything that comes from the vine nor drink wine or strong drink, nor eat any unclean thing; let her observe all that I commanded'" (Jdg. 13:8-14).

The Angel Ascended in the Flame of the Alter

"Then Manoah said to the angel of the Lord, 'Please let us detain you so that we may prepare a young goat for you.' The angel of the Lord said to Manoah, 'Though you detain me, I will not eat your food, but if you prepare a burnt offering, then offer it to the Lord.' For Manoah did not know that he was the angel of the Lord. Manoah said to the angel of the Lord, 'What is your name, so that when your words come to pass, we may honor you?' But the angel of the Lord said to him, 'Why do you ask my name, seeing it is wonderful?' So Manoah took the young goat with the grain offering and offered it on the rock to the Lord, and He performed wonders while Manoah and his wife looked on. For it came about when the flame went up from the altar toward heaven, that the angel of the Lord ascended in the flame of the altar. When Manoah and his wife saw this, they fell on their faces to the ground" (Jdg. 13:15-20).

The Angel Didn't Appear to Manoah or His Wife Again

"Now the angel of the Lord did not appear to Manoah or his wife again. Then Manoah knew that he was the angel of the Lord. So Manoah said to his wife, 'We will surely die, for we have seen God.' But his wife said to him, 'If the Lord had desired to kill us, He would not have accepted a burnt offering and a grain offering from our hands, nor would He have shown us all these things, nor would He have let us hear things like this at this time'" (Jdg. 13:21-23).

When the Angel Stretched out His Hand Toward Jerusalem to Destroy It, the Lord Relented

"So the Lord sent a pestilence upon Israel from the morning until the appointed time, and seventy thousand men of the people from Dan to Beersheba died. When the angel stretched out his hand toward

Jerusalem to destroy it, the Lord relented from the calamity and said to the angel who destroyed the people, 'It is enough! Now relax your hand!' And the angel of the Lord was by the threshing floor of Araunah the Jebusite. Then David spoke to the Lord when he saw the angel who was striking down the people, and said, 'Behold, it is I who have sinned, and it is I who have done wrong; but these sheep, what have they done? Please let Your hand be against me and against my father's house'" (2Sam. 24:15-17).

An Angel Spoke to Me

"Now an old prophet was living in Bethel; and his sons came and told him all the deeds which the man of God had done that day in Bethel; the words which he had spoken to the king, these also they related to their father. Their father said to them, 'Which way did he go?' Now his sons had seen the way which the man of God who came from Judah had gone. Then he said to his sons, 'Saddle the donkey for me.' So they saddled the donkey for him and he rode away on it. So he went after the man of God and found him sitting under an oak; and he said to him, 'Are you the man of God who came from Judah?' And he said, 'I am.' Then he said to him, 'Come home with me and eat bread.' He said, 'I cannot return with you, nor go with you, nor will I eat bread or drink water with you in this place. For a command came to me by the word of the Lord, "You shall eat no bread, nor drink water there; do not return by going the way which you came."' He said to him, 'I also am a prophet like you, and an angel spoke to me by the word of the Lord, saying, 'Bring him back with you to your house, that he may eat bread and drink water.'" But he lied to him. So he went back with him, and ate bread in his house and drank water" (1Ki.13:11-19).

Behold, There Was an Angel Touching Him

"Now Ahab told Jezebel all that Elijah had done, and how he had killed all the prophets with the sword. Then Jezebel sent a messenger to Elijah, saying, 'So may the gods do to me and even more, if I do not make your life as the life of one of them by tomorrow about this time.' And he was afraid and arose and ran for his life and came to Beersheba, which belongs to Judah, and left his servant there. But he himself went a day's journey into the wilderness, and came and sat down under a juniper tree; and he requested for himself that he might die, and said, 'It is enough; now, O Lord, take my life, for I am not better than my fathers.' He lay down and slept under a juniper tree; and behold, there was an angel touching him, and he said to him, 'Arise, eat.' Then he looked and behold, there was at his head a bread cake baked on hot stones, and a jar of water. So he ate and drank and lay down again. The angel of the Lord came again a second time and touched him and said, 'Arise, eat, because the journey is too great for you.' So he arose and ate and drank, and went in the strength of that food forty days and forty nights to Horeb, the mountain of God" (1Ki. 19:1-8).

The Angel Told Elijah to Deliver a Message

"Now Moab rebelled against Israel after the death of Ahab. And Ahaziah fell through the lattice in his upper chamber which was in Samaria, and became ill. So he sent messengers and said to them, 'Go, inquire of Baal-zebub, the god of Ekron, whether I will recover from this sickness.' But the angel of the Lord said to Elijah the Tishbite, 'Arise, go up to meet the messengers of the king of Samaria and say to them, "Is it because there is no God in Israel that you are going to inquire of Baal-zebub, the god of Ekron?" Now therefore thus says the Lord, "You shall not come down from the bed where you have gone up, but you shall surely die.'" Then Elijah departed" (2Ki. 1:1-4).

The Angel Told Elijah Not to Be Afraid

"So he again sent the captain of a third fifty with his fifty. When the third captain of fifty went up, he came and bowed down on his knees before Elijah, and begged him and said to him, 'O man of God, please let my life and the lives of these fifty servants of yours be precious in your sight. Behold fire came down from heaven and consumed the first two captains of fifty with their fifties; but now let my life be precious in your sight.' The angel of the Lord said to Elijah, 'Go down with him; do not be afraid of him.' So he arose and went down with him to the king. Then he said to him, 'Thus says the Lord, 'Because you have sent messengers to inquire of Baal-zebub, the god of Ekron—is it because there is no God in Israel to inquire of His word?— therefore you shall not come down from the bed where you have gone up, but shall surely die'''" (2 Ki.1:13-16).

The Angel Struck 185,000 and They Were All Dead

"Then it happened that night that the angel of the Lord went out and struck 185,000 in the camp of the Assyrians; and when men rose early in the morning, behold, all of them were dead. So Sennacherib king of Assyria departed and returned home, and lived at Nineveh. It came about as he was worshiping in the house of Nisroch his god, that Adrammelech and Sharezer killed him with the sword; and they escaped into the land of Ararat. And Esarhaddon his son became king in his place" (2Ki. 19:35-37).

The Angel Destroying Throughout All the Territory of Israel

"The Lord spoke to Gad, David's seer, saying, 'Go and speak to David, saying, 'Thus says the Lord, 'I offer you three things; choose for yourself one of them, which I will do to you.''' So Gad came to David and said to him, 'Thus says the Lord, "Take for yourself either three years of famine, or three months to be swept away before your foes, while the sword of your enemies overtakes you, or else three days of the sword of the Lord, even pestilence in the land, and the angel of the Lord destroying throughout all the territory of Israel." Now, therefore, consider what answer I shall return to Him who sent me.' David said to Gad, 'I am in great distress; please let me fall into the hand of the Lord, for His mercies are very great. But do not let me fall into the hand of man" (1Ch. 21:9-13).

God Sent an Angel to Jerusalem to Destroy It

"So the Lord sent a pestilence on Israel; 70,000 men of Israel fell. And God sent an angel to Jerusalem to destroy it; but as he was about to destroy it, the Lord saw and was sorry over the calamity, and said to the destroying angel, 'It is enough; now relax your hand.'

And the angel of the Lord was standing by the threshing floor of Ornan the Jebusite. Then David lifted up his eyes and saw the angel of the Lord standing between earth and heaven, with his drawn sword in his hand stretched out over Jerusalem. Then David and the elders, covered with sackcloth, fell on their faces. David said to God, 'Is it not I who commanded to count the people? Indeed, I am the one who has sinned and done very wickedly, but these sheep, what have they done? O Lord my God, please let Your hand be against me and my father's household, but not against Your people that they should be plagued'" (1Ch. 21:14-17).

The Lord Commanded the Angel, and He Put His Sword Back in Its Sheath

"Then the angel of the Lord commanded Gad to say to David, that David should go up and build an altar to the Lord on the threshing floor of Ornan the Jebusite. So David went up at the word of Gad, which he spoke in the name of the Lord. Now Ornan turned back and saw the angel, and his four sons who were with him hid themselves. And Ornan was threshing wheat. As David came to Ornan, Ornan looked and saw David, and went out from the threshing floor and prostrated himself before David with his face to the ground. Then David said to Ornan, 'Give me the site of this threshing floor, that I may build on it an altar to the Lord; for the full price you shall give it to me, that the plague may be restrained from the people.' Ornan said to David, 'Take it for yourself; and let my lord the king do what is good in his sight. See, I will give the oxen for burnt offerings and the threshing sledges for wood and the wheat for the grain offering; I will give it all.' But

King David said to Ornan, 'No, but I will surely buy it for the full price; for I will not take what is yours for the Lord, or offer a burnt offering which costs me nothing.' So David gave Ornan 600 shekels of gold by weight for the site. Then David built an altar to the Lord there and offered burnt offerings and peace offerings. And he called to the Lord and He answered him with fire from heaven on the altar of burnt offering. The Lord commanded the angel, and he put his sword back in its sheath" (1Ch. 21:18-27).

David Was Terrified by the Sword of the Angel

"At that time, when David saw that the Lord had answered him on the threshing floor of Ornan the Jebusite, he offered sacrifice there. For the tabernacle of the Lord, which Moses had made in the wilderness, and the altar of burnt offering were in the high place at Gibeon at that time. But David could not go before it to inquire of God, for he was terrified by the sword of the angel of the Lord" (1Ch. 21:28-30).

An Angel Destroyed Every Mighty Warrior, Commander and Officer in the Camp

"But King Hezekiah and Isaiah the prophet, the son of Amoz, prayed about this and cried out to heaven. And the Lord sent an angel who destroyed every mighty warrior, commander and officer in the camp of the king of Assyria. So he returned in shame to his own land. And when he had entered the temple of his god, some of his own children killed him there with the sword. So the Lord saved Hezekiah and the inhabitants of Jerusalem from the hand of Sennacherib the king of

Assyria and from the hand of all others, and guided them on every side. And many were bringing gifts to the Lord at Jerusalem and choice presents to Hezekiah king of Judah, so that he was exalted in the sight of all nations thereafter" (2Ch. 32:20-23).

The Angel of the Lord Encamps Around Those Who Fear Him and He Rescues Them

"I sought the Lord, and He answered me, And delivered me from all my fears. They looked to Him and were radiant, And their faces will never be ashamed. This poor man cried, and the Lord heard him And saved him out of all his troubles. The angel of the Lord encamps around those who fear Him, And rescues them" (Ps. 34:4-7).

With the Angel of the Lord Driving Them On

"Contend, O Lord, with those who contend with me; Fight against those who fight against me. Take hold of buckler and shield And rise up for my help. Draw also the spear and the battle-axe to meet those who pursue me; Say to my soul, 'I am your salvation.' Let those be ashamed and dishonored who seek my life; Let those be turned back and humiliated who devise evil against me. Let them be like chaff before the wind, With the angel of the Lord driving them on. Let their way be dark and slippery, With the angel of the Lord pursuing them. For without cause they hid their net for me; Without cause they dug a pit for my soul. Let destruction come upon him unawares, And let the net which he hid catch himself; Into that very destruction let him fall. And my soul shall rejoice in the Lord; It shall exult in His salvation" (Ps. 35:1-9).

The Angel Struck 185,000 in the Camp of the Assyrians

"Then the angel of the Lord went out and struck 185,000 in the camp of the Assyrians; and when men arose early in the morning, behold, all of these were dead. So Sennacherib king of Assyria departed and returned home and lived at Nineveh. It came about as he was worshiping in the house of Nisroch his god, that Adrammelech and Sharezer his sons killed him with the sword; and they escaped into the land of Ararat. And Esarhaddon his son became king in his place" (Is. 37:36-38).

The Angel of His Presence Saved Them

"I shall make mention of the lovingkindnesses of the Lord, the praises of the Lord, According to all that the Lord has granted us, And the great goodness toward the house of Israel, Which He has granted them according to His compassion And according to the abundance of His lovingkindnesses. For He said, 'Surely, they are My people, Sons who will not deal falsely.' So He became their Savior. In all their affliction He was afflicted, And the angel of His presence saved them; In His love and in His mercy He redeemed them, And He lifted them and carried them all the days of old. But they rebelled And grieved His Holy Spirit; Therefore He turned Himself to become their enemy, He fought against them. Then His people remembered the days of old, of Moses. Where is He who brought them up out of the sea with the shepherds of His flock?

Where is He who put His Holy Spirit in the midst of them, Who caused His glorious arm to go at the right hand of Moses, Who divided the waters before them to make for Himself an everlasting name, Who led them through the depths? Like the horse in the wilderness, they did not stumble; As the cattle which go down into the valley, The Spirit of the Lord gave them rest. So You led Your people, To make for Yourself a glorious name" (Is. 63:7-14).

Sent His Angel and Delivered His Servants

"Nebuchadnezzar responded and said, 'Blessed be the God of Shadrach, Meshach and Abed-nego, who has sent His angel and delivered His servants who put their trust in Him, violating the king's command, and yielded up their bodies so as not to serve or worship any god except their own God. Therefore I make a decree that any people, nation or tongue that speaks anything offensive against the God of Shadrach, Meshach and Abed-nego shall be torn limb from limb and their houses reduced to a rubbish heap, inasmuch as there is no other god who is able to deliver in this way.' Then the king caused Shadrach, Meshach and Abed-nego to prosper in the province of Babylon" (Da. 3:28-30).

God Sent His Angel to Shut the Lions' Mouth

"Then the king arose at dawn, at the break of day, and went in haste to the lions' den. When he had come near the den to Daniel, he cried out with a troubled voice. The king spoke and said to Daniel, 'Daniel, servant of the living God, has your God, whom you constantly serve, been able to deliver you from the lions?' Then Daniel spoke to the king, 'O king, live forever! My God sent His angel and shut the lions' mouths and they have not harmed me, inasmuch as I was found innocent before Him; and also toward you, O king, I have committed no crime.' Then the king was very pleased and gave orders for Daniel to be taken up out of the den. So Daniel was taken up out of the den and no injury whatever was found on him, because he had trusted in his God. The king then gave orders, and they brought those men who had maliciously accused Daniel, and they cast them, their children and their wives into the lions' den; and they had not reached the bottom of the den before the lions overpowered them and crushed all their bones" (Da. 6:19-24).

He Wrestled with the Angel

"Ephraim feeds on wind, And pursues the east wind continually; He multiplies lies and violence. Moreover, he makes a covenant with Assyria, And oil is carried to Egypt. The Lord also has a dispute with Judah, And will punish Jacob according to his ways; He will repay him according to his deeds. In the womb he took his brother by the heel, And in his maturity he contended with God. Yes, he wrestled with the angel and prevailed; He wept and sought His favor. He found Him at Bethel And there He spoke with us, Even the Lord, the God of hosts, The Lord is His name. Therefore, return to your God, Observe kindness and justice, And wait for your God continually. A merchant, in whose hands are false balances, He loves to oppress. And Ephraim said, 'Surely I have become rich, I have found wealth for myself; In all my labors they will find in me

No iniquity, which would be sin.' But I have been the Lord your God since the land of Egypt; I will make you live in tents again, As in the days of the appointed festival. I have also spoken to the prophets, And I gave numerous visions, And through the prophets I gave parables. Is there iniquity in Gilead? Surely they are worthless. In Gilgal they sacrifice bulls, Yes, their altars are like the stone heaps Beside the furrows of the field" (Ho. 12:1-11).

The Angel Said, "We Have Patrolled the Earth."

"On the twenty-fourth day of the eleventh month, which is the month Shebat, in the second year of Darius, the word of the Lord came to Zechariah the prophet, the son of Berechiah, the son of Iddo, as follows: I saw at night, and behold, a man was riding on a red horse, and he was standing among the myrtle trees which were in the ravine, with red, sorrel and white horses behind him. Then I said, 'My lord, what are these?' And the angel who was speaking with me said to me, 'I will show you what these are.' And the man who was standing among the myrtle trees answered and said, 'These are those whom the Lord has sent to patrol the earth.' So they answered the angel of the Lord who was standing among the myrtle trees and said, 'We have patrolled the earth, and behold, all the earth is peaceful and quiet'" (Zec. 1:7-11).

The Angel of the Lord

"Then the angel of the Lord said, 'O Lord of hosts, how long will You have no compassion for Jerusalem and the cities of Judah, with which You have been indignant these seventy years?' The Lord answered the angel who was speaking with me with gracious words, comforting words. So the angel who was speaking with me said to me, 'Proclaim, saying, 'Thus says the Lord of hosts, 'I am exceedingly jealous for Jerusalem and Zion. But I am very angry with the nations who are at ease; for while I was only a little angry, they furthered the disaster.' Therefore thus says the Lord, 'I will return to Jerusalem with compassion; My house will be built in it,' declares the Lord of hosts, 'and a measuring line will be stretched over Jerusalem.'' Again, proclaim, saying, 'Thus says the Lord of hosts, 'My cities will again overflow with prosperity, and the Lord will again comfort Zion and again choose Jerusalem''''' (Zec. 1:12-17).

ANGELS IN THE OLD TESTAMENT

The Two Angels Came to Sodom in the Evening

"Now the two angels came to Sodom in the evening as Lot was sitting in the gate of Sodom. When Lot saw them, he rose to meet them and bowed down with his face to the ground. And he said, 'Now behold, my lords, please turn aside into your servant's house, and spend the night, and wash your feet; then you may rise early and go on your way.' They said however, 'No, but we shall spend the night in the square.' Yet he urged them strongly, so they turned aside to him and entered his house; and he prepared a feast for them, and baked unleavened bread, and they ate. Before they lay down, the men of the city, the men of Sodom, surrounded the house, both young and old, all the people from every quarter; and they called to Lot and said to him, 'Where are the men who came to you tonight? Bring them out to us that we may have relations with them.' But Lot went out to them at the doorway, and shut the door behind him, and said, 'Please, my brothers, do not act wickedly. Now behold, I have two daughters who have not had relations with man; please let me bring them out to you, and do to them whatever you like; only do nothing to these men, inasmuch as they have come under the shelter of my roof.' But they said, 'Stand aside.' Furthermore, they said, 'This one came in as an alien, and already he is acting like a judge; now we will treat you worse than them.' So they pressed hard against Lot and came near to break the door. But the men reached out their hands and brought Lot into the house with them, and shut the door. And they struck the men who were at the doorway of the house with blindness, both small and great, so that they wearied themselves trying to find the doorway" (Ge. 19:1-11).

When Morning Dawned, the Angels Urged Lot

"And when morning dawned, the angels urged Lot, saying, 'Up, take your wife and your two daughters, who are here, lest you be swept away in the punishment of the city.' But he hesitated. So the men seized his hand and the hand of his wife and the hands of his two daughters, for the compassion of the Lord was upon him; and they brought him out, and put him outside the city. And it came about when they had brought them outside, that one said, 'Escape for your life! Do not look behind you, and do not stay anywhere in the valley; escape to the mountains, lest you be swept away.' But Lot said to them, 'Oh no, my lords! Now behold, your servant has found favor in your sight, and you have magnified your lovingkindness, which you have shown me by saving my life; but I cannot escape to the mountains, lest the disaster overtake me and I die; now behold, this town is near enough to flee to, and it is small. Please, let me escape there (is it not small?) that my life may be saved.' And he said to him, 'Behold, I grant you this request also, not to overthrow the town of which you have spoken. Hurry, escape there, for I cannot do anything until you arrive there.' Therefore the name of the town was called Zoar" (Ge. 19:15-22).

The Angels of God Were Ascending and Descending

"Then Jacob departed from Beersheba and went toward Haran. And he came to a certain place and spent the night there, because the sun had set; and he took one of the stones of the place and put it under his head, and lay down in that place. And he had a dream, and behold, a ladder was set on the earth with its top reaching to heaven; and behold, the angels of God were ascending and descending on it. And behold, the Lord stood above it and said, 'I am the Lord, the God of your father Abraham and the God of Isaac; the land on which you lie, I will give it to you and to your descendants. Your descendants shall also be like the dust of the earth, and you shall spread out to the west and to the east and to the north and to the south; and in you and in your descendants shall all the families of the earth be blessed. And behold, I am with you, and will keep you wherever you go, and will bring you back to this land; for I will not leave you until I have done what I have promised you.' Then Jacob awoke from his sleep and said, 'Surely the Lord is in this place, and I did not know it.' And he was afraid and said, 'How awesome is this place! This is none other than the house of God, and this is the gate of heaven'" (Ge. 28:10-17).

The Angels of God Met Him

"Now as Jacob went on his way, the angels of God met him. And Jacob said when he saw them, 'This is God's camp.' So he named that place Mahanaim" (Ge. 32:1-2).

Against His Angels He Charges Error

"Now a word was brought to me stealthily, And my ear received a whisper of it. Amid disquieting thoughts from the visions of the night, When deep sleep falls on men, dread came upon me, and trembling, And made all my bones shake. Then a spirit passed by my face; the hair of my flesh bristled up. It stood still, but I could not discern its appearance; A form was before my eyes; there was silence, then I heard a voice: 'Can mankind be just before God? Can a man be pure before his Maker? He puts no trust even in His servants; And against His angels He charges error. How much more those who dwell in houses of clay, Whose foundation is in the dust, Who are crushed before the moth! Between morning and evening they are broken in pieces; Unobserved, they perish forever. Is not their tent-cord plucked up within them? They die, yet without wisdom'" (Job 4:12-21).

A Band of Destroying Angels

"How often they rebelled against Him in the wilderness, And grieved Him in the desert! And again and again they tempted God, And pained the Holy One of Israel. They did not remember His power, The day when He redeemed them from the adversary, When He performed His signs in Egypt, And His marvels in the field of Zoan, and turned their rivers to blood, and their streams, they could not drink. He sent among them swarms of flies, which devoured them, And frogs which destroyed them. He gave also their crops to the grasshopper, and the product of their labor to the locust. He destroyed their vines with hailstones, and their sycamore trees with frost. He gave over their cattle also to the hailstones, and their herds to bolts of lightning. He sent upon them His burning anger, fury, and indignation, and trouble, a band of destroying angels. He leveled a path for His anger; He did not spare their soul from death, but gave over their life to the plague, and smote all the first-born in Egypt, The first issue of their virility in the tents of Ham. But He led forth His own people like sheep, and guided them in the wilderness like a flock; and He led them safely, so that they did not fear; but the sea engulfed their enemies" (Ps 78:40-53).

He Will Give His Angels Charge Concerning You

"For He will give His angels charge concerning you, to guard you in all your ways. They will bear you up in their hands, lest you strike your foot against a stone. You will tread upon the lion and cobra, the young lion and the serpent you will trample down" (Ps. 91:11-13).

You His Angels, Mighty in Strength, Who Perform His Word

"The Lord has established His throne in the heavens; and His sovereignty rules over all. Bless the Lord, you His angels, mighty in strength, who perform His word, obeying the voice of His word! Bless the Lord, all you His hosts, you who serve Him, doing His will. Bless the Lord, all you works of His, in all places of His dominion; bless the Lord, O my soul" (Ps. 103:19-22)!

Praise Him, All His Angels; Praise Him, All His Hosts

"Praise the Lord! Praise the Lord from the heavens; praise Him in the heights! Praise Him, all His angels; praise Him, all His hosts! Praise Him, sun and moon; praise Him, all stars of light! Praise Him, highest heavens, and the waters that are above the heavens!

Let them praise the name of the Lord, for He commanded and they were created. He has also established them forever and ever; He has made a decree which will not pass away" (Ps. 148:1-6).

ANGEL IN THE NEW TESTAMENT

An Angel of the Lord Appeared to Him in a Dream

"Now the birth of Jesus Christ was as follows: when His mother Mary had been betrothed to Joseph, before they came together she was found to be with child by the Holy Spirit. And Joseph her husband, being a righteous man and not wanting to disgrace her, planned to send her away secretly. But when he had considered this, behold, an angel of the Lord appeared to him in a dream, saying, 'Joseph, son of David, do not be afraid to take Mary as your wife; for the Child who has been conceived in her is of the Holy Spirit. She will bear a Son; and you shall call His name Jesus, for He will save His people from their sins.' Now all this took place to fulfill what was spoken by the Lord through the prophet: 'BEHOLD, THE VIRGIN SHALL BE WITH CHILD AND SHALL BEAR A SON, AND THEY SHALL CALL HIS NAME IMMANUEL,' which translated means, 'GOD WITH US.' And Joseph awoke from his sleep and did as the angel of the Lord commanded him, and took Mary as his wife, but kept her a virgin until she gave birth to a Son; and he called His name Jesus" (Mt. 1:18-25).

The Angel Told Joseph, "Take the Child and His Mother and Flee."

"Now when they had gone, behold, an angel of the Lord appeared to Joseph in a dream and said, 'Get up! Take the Child and His mother and flee to Egypt, and remain there until I tell you; for Herod is going to search for the Child to destroy Him.' So Joseph got up and took the Child and His mother while it was still night, and left for Egypt" (Mt. 2:13-14).

The Angel Said, "Go to Israel; for Those Who Sought the Child's Life Are Dead."

"But when Herod died, behold, an angel of the Lord appeared in a dream to Joseph in Egypt, and said, 'Get up, take the Child and His mother, and go into the land of Israel; for those who sought the Child's life are dead.' So Joseph got up, took the Child and His mother, and came into the land of Israel. But when he heard that Archelaus was reigning over Judea in place of his father Herod, he was afraid to go there. Then after being warned by God in a dream, he left for the regions of Galilee, and came and lived in a city called Nazareth. This was to fulfill what was spoken through the prophets: 'He shall be called a Nazarene'" (Mt. 2:19-23).

An Angel Descended from Heaven and Came and Rolled Away the Stone

"Now after the Sabbath, as it began to dawn toward the first day of the week, Mary Magdalene and the other Mary came to look at the grave. And behold, a severe earthquake had occurred, for an angel of the Lord descended from heaven and came and rolled away the stone and sat upon it. And his appearance was like lightning, and his clothing as white as snow. The guards shook for fear of him and became like dead men. The angel said to the women, 'Do not be afraid; for I know that you are looking for Jesus who has been crucified. He is not here, for He has risen, just as He said. Come, see the place where He was lying. Go quickly and tell His disciples that He has risen from the dead; and behold, He is going ahead of you into Galilee, there you will see Him; behold, I have told you'" (Mt. 28:1-7).

Zacharias was Troubled When He Saw the Angel, and Fear Gripped Him

"Now it happened that while he was performing his priestly service before God in the appointed order of his division, according to the custom of the priestly office, he was chosen by lot to enter the temple of the Lord and burn incense. And the whole multitude of the people were in prayer outside at the hour of the incense offering. And an angel of the Lord appeared to him, standing to the right of the altar of incense. Zacharias was troubled when he saw the angel, and fear gripped him. But the angel said to him, 'Do not be afraid, Zacharias, for your petition has been heard, and your wife Elizabeth will bear you a son, and you will give him the name John. You will have joy and gladness, and many will rejoice at his birth. For he will be great in the sight of the Lord; and he will drink no wine or liquor, and he will be filled with the Holy Spirit while yet in his mother's womb. And he will turn many of the sons of Israel back to the Lord their God. It is he who will go as a forerunner before Him in the spirit and power of Elijah, TO TURN THE HEARTS OF THE FATHERS BACK TO THE CHILDREN, and the disobedient to the attitude of the righteous, so as to make ready a people prepared for the Lord'" (Lk. 1:8-17).

Chapter Four

The Angel Was Sent to Bring Good News

"Zacharias said to the angel, 'How will I know this for certain? For I am an old man and my wife is advanced in years.' The angel answered and said to him, 'I am Gabriel, who stands in the presence of God, and I have been sent to speak to you and to bring you this good news. And behold, you shall be silent and unable to speak until the day when these things take place, because you did not believe my words, which will be fulfilled in their proper time'" (Lk. 1:18-20).

The Angel Said to Her, "Do Not be Afraid, Mary; for You Have Found Favor with God

"Now in the sixth month the angel Gabriel was sent from God to a city in Galilee called Nazareth, to a virgin engaged to a man whose name was Joseph, of the descendants of David; and the virgin's name was Mary. And coming in, he said to her, 'Greetings, favored one! The Lord is with you.' But she was very perplexed at this statement, and kept pondering what kind of salutation this was. The angel said to her, 'Do not be afraid, Mary; for you have found favor with God. And behold, you will conceive in your womb and bear a son, and you shall name Him Jesus. He will be great and will be called the Son of the Most High; and the Lord God will give Him the throne of His father David; and He will reign over the house of Jacob forever, and His kingdom will have no end.' Mary said to the angel, 'How can this be, since I am a virgin?' The angel answered and said to her, 'The Holy Spirit will come upon you, and the power of the Most High will overshadow you; and for that reason the holy Child shall be called the Son of God. And behold, even your relative Elizabeth has also conceived a son in her old age; and she who was called barren is now in her sixth month. For nothing will be impossible with God.' And Mary said, 'Behold, the bondslave of the Lord; may it be done to me according to your word.' And the angel departed from her" (Lk. 1:26-38).

An Angel Suddenly Stood Before Them, and the Glory of the Lord Shone Around Them

"In the same region there were some shepherds staying out in the fields and keeping watch over their flock by night. And an angel of the Lord suddenly stood before them, and the glory of the Lord shone around them; and they were terribly frightened. But the angel said to them, 'Do not be afraid; for behold, I bring you good news of great joy which will be for all the people; for today in the city of David there has been born for you a Savior, who is Christ the Lord. This will be a sign for you: you will find a baby wrapped in cloths and lying in a manger.' And suddenly there appeared with the angel a multitude of the heavenly host praising God and saying, 'Glory to God in the highest, And on earth peace among men with whom He is pleased'" (Lk. 2:8-14).

The Name Given by the Angel

"And when eight days had passed, before His circumcision, His name was then called Jesus, the name given by the angel before He was conceived in the womb" (Lk. 2:21).

An Angel from Heaven Appeared to Him, Strengthening Him

"And He came out and proceeded as was His custom to the Mount of Olives; and the disciples also followed Him. When He arrived at the place, He said to them, 'Pray that you may not enter into temptation.' And He withdrew from them about a stone's throw, and He knelt down and began to pray, saying, 'Father, if You are willing, remove this cup from Me; yet not My will, but Yours be done.' Now an angel from heaven appeared to Him, strengthening Him. And being in agony He was praying very fervently; and His sweat became like drops of blood, falling down upon the ground. When He rose from prayer, He came to the disciples and found them sleeping from sorrow, and said to them, 'Why are you sleeping? Get up and pray that you may not enter into temptation'" (Lk. 22:39-46).

An Angel of the Lord Went Down at Certain Seasons

"Now there is in Jerusalem by the sheep gate a pool, which is called in Hebrew Bethesda, having five porticoes. In these lay a multitude of those who were sick, blind, lame, and withered, [[waiting for the moving of the waters; for an angel of the Lord went down at certain seasons into the pool and stirred up the water; whoever then first, after the stirring up of the water, stepped in was made well from whatever disease with which he was afflicted.]] A man was there who had been ill for thirty-eight years. When Jesus saw him lying there, and knew that he had already been a long time in that condition, He said to him, 'Do you wish to get well?' The sick man answered Him, 'Sir, I have no man to put me into the pool when the water is stirred up, but while I am coming, another steps down before me.' Jesus said to him, 'Get up, pick up your pallet and walk.' Immediately the man became well, and picked up his pallet and began to walk. Now it was the Sabbath on that day. So the Jews were saying to the man who was cured, 'It is the Sabbath, and it is not permissible for you to carry your pallet.' But he answered them, 'He who made me well was the one who said to me, 'Pick up your pallet and walk.''' They asked him, 'Who is the man who said to you, "Pick up your pallet and walk"?' But the man who was healed did not know who it was, for Jesus had slipped away while there was a crowd in that place. Afterward Jesus found him in the temple and said to him, 'Behold, you have become well; do not sin anymore, so that nothing worse happens to you.' The man went away, and told the Jews that it was Jesus who had made him well. For this reason the Jews were persecuting Jesus, because He was doing these things on the Sabbath. But He answered them, 'My Father is working until now, and I Myself am working.' For this reason therefore the Jews were seeking all the more to kill Him, because He not only was breaking the Sabbath, but also was calling God His own Father, making Himself equal with God" (Jn. 5:2-18).

Others Were Saying, "An Angel Has Spoken to Him."

"'Now My soul has become troubled; and what shall I say, "Father, save Me from this hour"? But for this purpose I came to this hour. Father, glorify Your name.' Then a voice came out of heaven: 'I have both glorified it, and will glorify it again.' So the crowd of people who stood by and heard it were saying that it had thundered; others were saying, 'An angel has spoken to Him.' Jesus answered and said, 'This voice has not come for My sake, but for your sakes. Now judgment is upon this world; now the ruler of this world will be cast out. And I, if I am lifted up from the earth, will draw all men to Myself.' But He was saying this to indicate the kind of death by which He was to die. The crowd then answered Him, 'We have heard out of the Law that the Christ is to remain forever; and how can You say, 'The Son of Man must be lifted up'? Who is this Son of Man?' So Jesus said to them, 'For a little while longer the Light is among you. Walk while you have the Light, so that darkness will not overtake you; he who walks in the darkness does not know where he goes. While you have the Light, believe in the Light, so that you may become sons of Light.' These things Jesus spoke, and He went away and hid Himself from them. But though He had performed so many signs before them, yet they were not believing in Him. This was to fulfill the word of Isaiah the prophet which he spoke: 'LORD, WHO HAS BELIEVED OUR REPORT? AND TO WHOM HAS THE ARM OF THE LORD BEEN REVEALED?' For this reason they could not believe, for Isaiah said again, 'HE HAS BLINDED THEIR EYES AND HE HARDENED THEIR HEART, SO THAT THEY WOULD NOT SEE WITH THEIR EYES AND PERCEIVE WITH THEIR HEART, AND BE CONVERTED AND I HEAL THEM.' These things Isaiah said because he saw His glory, and he spoke of Him. Nevertheless many even of the rulers believed in Him, but because of the Pharisees they were not confessing Him, for fear that they would be put out of the synagogue; for they loved the approval of men rather than the approval of God" (Jn. 12:27-43).

An Angel of the Lord Opened the Gates of the Prison

"But the high priest rose up, along with all his associates (that is the sect of the Sadducees), and they were filled with jealousy. They laid hands on the apostles and put them in a public jail. But during the night an angel of the Lord opened the gates of the prison, and taking them out he said, 'Go, stand and speak to the people in the temple the whole message of this Life.' Upon hearing this, they entered into the temple about daybreak and began to teach. Now when the high priest and his associates came, they called the Council together, even all the Senate of the sons of Israel, and sent orders to the prison house for them to be brought. But the officers who came did not find them in the prison; and they returned and reported back, saying, 'We found the prison house locked quite securely and the guards standing at the doors; but when we had opened up, we found no one inside.' Now when the captain of the temple guard and the chief priests heard these words, they were greatly perplexed about them as to what would come of this. But someone came and reported to them, 'The men whom you put in prison are standing in the temple and teaching the people!' Then the captain went along with the officers and proceeded to bring them back without violence (for they were afraid of the people, that they might be stoned)" (Ac. 5:17-26).

They Saw His Face Like the Face of an Angel

"And Stephen, full of grace and power, was performing great wonders and signs among the people. But some men from what was called the Synagogue of the Freedmen, including both Cyrenians and Alexandrians, and some from Cilicia and Asia, rose up and argued with Stephen. But they were unable to cope with the wisdom and the Spirit with which he was speaking. Then they secretly induced men to say, 'We have heard him speak blasphemous words against Moses and against God.' And they stirred up the people, the elders and the scribes, and they came up to him and dragged him away and brought him before the Council. They put forward false witnesses who said, 'This man incessantly speaks against this holy place and the Law; for we have heard him say that this Nazarene, Jesus, will destroy this place and alter the customs which Moses handed down to us.' And fixing their gaze on him, all who were sitting in the Council saw his face like the face of an angel" (Ac. 6:8-15).

An Angel Appeared to Him in the Wilderness of Mount Sinai

"After forty years had passed, AN ANGEL APPEARED TO HIM IN THE WILDERNESS OF MOUNT Sinai, IN THE FLAME OF A BURNING THORN BUSH. When Moses saw it, he marveled at the sight; and as he approached to look more closely, there came the voice of the Lord: 'I AM THE GOD OF YOUR FATHERS, THE GOD OF ABRAHAM AND ISAAC AND JACOB.' Moses shook with fear and would not venture to look. BUT THE LORD SAID TO HIM, 'TAKE OFF THE SANDALS FROM YOUR FEET, FOR THE PLACE ON WHICH YOU ARE STANDING IS HOLY GROUND. I HAVE CERTAINLY SEEN THE OPPRESSION OF MY PEOPLE IN EGYPT AND HAVE HEARD THEIR GROANS, AND I HAVE COME

DOWN TO RESCUE THEM; COME NOW, AND I WILL SEND YOU TO EGYPT'"'" (Ac. 7:30-34).

The Angel Who Appeared to Him in the Thorn Bush

"This Moses whom they disowned, saying, 'WHO MADE YOU A RULER AND A JUDGE?' is the one whom God sent to be both a ruler and a deliverer with the help of the angel who appeared to him in the thorn bush. This man led them out, performing wonders and signs in the land of Egypt and in the Red Sea and in the wilderness for forty years. This is the Moses who said to the sons of Israel, 'GOD WILL RAISE UP FOR YOU A PROPHET LIKE ME FROM YOUR BRETHREN.' This is the one who was in the congregation in the wilderness together with the angel who was speaking to him on Mount Sinai, and who was with our fathers; and he received living oracles to pass on to you. Our fathers were unwilling to be obedient to him, but repudiated him and in their hearts turned back to Egypt, SAYING TO AARON, 'MAKE FOR US GODS WHO WILL GO BEFORE US; FOR THIS MOSES WHO LED US OUT OF THE LAND OF EGYPT — WE DO NOT KNOW WHAT HAPPENED TO HIM.' At that time they made a calf and brought a sacrifice to the idol, and were rejoicing in the works of their hands. But God turned away and delivered them up to serve the host of heaven; as it is written in the book of the prophets, 'IT WAS NOT TO ME THAT YOU OFFERED VICTIMS AND SACRIFICES FORTY YEARS IN THE WILDERNESS, WAS IT, O HOUSE OF ISRAEL? YOU ALSO TOOK ALONG THE TABERNACLE OF MOLOCH AND THE STAR OF THE GOD ROMPHA, THE IMAGES WHICH YOU MADE TO WORSHIP. I

ALSO WILL REMOVE YOU BEYOND BABYLON'"
(Ac. 7:35-43).

An Angel of the Lord Spoke to Philip

"But an angel of the Lord spoke to Philip saying, 'Get up and go south to the road that descends from Jerusalem to Gaza.' (This is a desert road.) So he got up and went; and there was an Ethiopian eunuch, a court official of Candace, queen of the Ethiopians, who was in charge of all her treasure; and he had come to Jerusalem to worship, and he was returning and sitting in his chariot, and was reading the prophet Isaiah. Then the Spirit said to Philip, 'Go up and join this chariot.' Philip ran up and heard him reading Isaiah the prophet, and said, 'Do you understand what you are reading?' And he said, 'Well, how could I, unless someone guides me?' And he invited Philip to come up and sit with him. Now the passage of Scripture which he was reading was this: 'HE WAS LED AS A SHEEP TO SLAUGHTER; AND AS A LAMB BEFORE ITS SHEARER IS SILENT, SO HE DOES NOT OPEN HIS MOUTH. IN HUMILIATION HIS JUDGMENT WAS TAKEN AWAY; WHO WILL RELATE HIS GENERATION? FOR HIS LIFE IS REMOVED FROM THE EARTH.' The eunuch answered Philip and said, 'Please tell me, of whom does the prophet say this? Of himself or of someone else?' Then Philip opened his mouth, and beginning from this Scripture he preached Jesus to him. As they went along the road they came to some water; and the eunuch said, 'Look! Water! What prevents me from being baptized?' [[And Philip said, 'If you believe with all your heart, you may.' And he answered and said, 'I believe that Jesus Christ is the Son of God.']]

And he ordered the chariot to stop; and they both went down into the water, Philip as well as the eunuch, and he baptized him. When they came up out of the water, the Spirit of the Lord snatched Philip away; and the eunuch no longer saw him, but went on his way rejoicing. But Philip found himself at Azotus, and as he passed through he kept preaching the gospel to all the cities until he came to Caesarea" (Ac. 8:26-40).

Cornelius Saw an Angel in a Vision

"Now there was a man at Caesarea named Cornelius, a centurion of what was called the Italian cohort, a devout man and one who feared God with all his household, and gave many alms to the Jewish people and prayed to God continually. About the ninth hour of the day he clearly saw in a vision an angel of God who had just come in and said to him, 'Cornelius!' And fixing his gaze on him and being much alarmed, he said, 'What is it, Lord?' And he said to him, 'Your prayers and alms have ascended as a memorial before God. Now dispatch some men to Joppa and send for a man named Simon, who is also called Peter; he is staying with a tanner named Simon, whose house is by the sea.' When the angel who was speaking to him had left, he summoned two of his servants and a devout soldier of those who were his personal attendants, and after he had explained everything to them, he sent them to Joppa" (Ac. 10:1-8).

Directed by a Holy Angel

"Now while Peter was greatly perplexed in mind as to what the vision which he had seen might be, behold, the men who had been sent by Cornelius, having asked directions for Simon's house, appeared at the gate; and calling out, they were asking whether Simon, who was also called Peter, was staying there. While Peter was reflecting on the vision, the Spirit said to him, 'Behold, three men are looking for you. But get up, go downstairs and accompany them without misgivings, for I have sent them Myself.' Peter went down to the men and said, 'Behold, I am the one you are looking for; what is the reason for which you have come?' They said, 'Cornelius, a centurion, a righteous and God-fearing man well spoken of by the entire nation of the Jews, was divinely directed by a holy angel to send for you to come to his house and hear a message from you.' So he invited them in and gave them lodging. And on the next day he got up and went away with them, and some of the brethren from Joppa accompanied him. On the following day he entered Caesarea. Now Cornelius was waiting for them and had called together his relatives and close friends. When Peter entered, Cornelius met him, and fell at his feet and worshiped him. But Peter raised him up, saying, 'Stand up; I too am just a man.' As he talked with him, he entered and found many people assembled. And he said to them, 'You yourselves know how unlawful it is for a man who is a Jew to associate with a foreigner or to visit him; and yet God has shown me that I should not call any man unholy or unclean. That is why I came without even raising any objection when I was sent for. So I ask for what reason you have sent for me'" (Ac. 10:17-29).

The Angel Said, "Send to Joppa for Simon Who is Called Peter."

"Now the apostles and the brethren who were throughout Judea heard that the Gentiles also had received the word of God. And when Peter came up to Jerusalem, those who were circumcised took issue with him, saying, 'You went to uncircumcised men and ate with them.' But Peter began speaking and proceeded to explain to them in orderly sequence, saying, 'I was in the city of Joppa praying; and in a trance I saw a vision, an object coming down like a great sheet lowered by four corners from the sky; and it came right down to me, and when I had fixed my gaze on it and was observing it I saw the four-footed animals of the earth and the wild beasts and the crawling creatures and the birds of the air. I also heard a voice saying to me, 'Get up, Peter; kill and eat." But I said, "By no means, Lord, for nothing unholy or unclean has ever entered my mouth." But a voice from heaven answered a second time, "What God has cleansed, no longer consider unholy." This happened three times, and everything was drawn back up into the sky. And behold, at that moment three men appeared at the house in which we were staying, having been sent to me from Caesarea. The Spirit told me to go with them without misgivings. These six brethren also went with me and we entered the man's house. And he reported to us how he had seen the angel standing in his house, and saying, "Send to Joppa and have Simon, who is also called Peter, brought here; and he will speak words to you by which you will be saved, you and all your household." And as I began to speak, the Holy Spirit fell upon them just as He did upon us at the beginning. And I remembered the word of the Lord, how He used to say, "John baptized with water, but you will be baptized with the Holy Spirit." Therefore if God gave to them the same gift as He gave to us also after believing in the Lord Jesus Christ, who was I that I could stand in God's way?' When they heard this, they quieted down and glorified God, saying, 'Well then, God has granted to the Gentiles also the repentance that leads to life'" (Ac. 11:1-18).

The Angel in the Prison Cell Told Peter, "Get Up Quickly."

"On the very night when Herod was about to bring him forward, Peter was sleeping between two soldiers, bound with two chains, and guards in front of the door were watching over the prison. And behold, an angel of the Lord suddenly appeared and a light shone in the cell; and he struck Peter's side and woke him up, saying, 'Get up quickly.' And his chains fell off his hands. And the angel said to him, 'Gird yourself and put on your sandals.' And he did so. And he said to him, 'Wrap your cloak around you and follow me.' And he went out and continued to follow, and he did not know that what was being done by the angel was real, but thought he was seeing a vision. When they had passed the first and second guard, they came to the iron gate that leads into the city, which opened for them by itself; and they went out and went along one street, and immediately the angel departed from him. When Peter came to himself, he said, 'Now I know for sure that the Lord has sent forth His angel and rescued me from the hand of Herod and from all that the Jewish people were expecting.' And when he realized this, he went to the house of Mary, the mother of John who was also called

Mark, where many were gathered together and were praying. When he knocked at the door of the gate, a servant-girl named Rhoda came to answer. When she recognized Peter's voice, because of her joy she did not open the gate, but ran in and announced that Peter was standing in front of the gate. They said to her, 'You are out of your mind!' But she kept insisting that it was so. They kept saying, 'It is his angel.' But Peter continued knocking; and when they had opened the door, they saw him and were amazed. But motioning to them with his hand to be silent, he described to them how the Lord had led him out of the prison. And he said, 'Report these things to James and the brethren.' Then he left and went to another place" (Ac. 12:6-17).

An Angel of the Lord Struck Him Because He Did Not Give God the Glory

"Now he was very angry with the people of Tyre and Sidon; and with one accord they came to him, and having won over Blastus the king's chamberlain, they were asking for peace, because their country was fed by the king's country. On an appointed day Herod, having put on his royal apparel, took his seat on the rostrum and began delivering an address to them. The people kept crying out, 'The voice of a god and not of a man!' And immediately an angel of the Lord struck him because he did not give God the glory, and he was eaten by worms and died" (Ac. 12:20-23).

The Sadducees Say that There Is No Resurrection, nor an Angel, nor a Spirit

"But perceiving that one group were Sadducees and the other Pharisees, Paul began crying out in the Council, 'Brethren, I am a Pharisee, a son of Pharisees; I am on trial for the hope and resurrection of the dead!' As he said this, there occurred a dissension between the Pharisees and Sadducees, and the assembly was divided. For the Sadducees say that there is no resurrection, nor an angel, nor a spirit, but the Pharisees acknowledge them all. And there occurred a great uproar; and some of the scribes of the Pharisaic party stood up and began to argue heatedly, saying, 'We find nothing wrong with this man; suppose a spirit or an angel has spoken to him?' And as a great dissension was developing, the commander was afraid Paul would be torn to pieces by them and ordered the troops to go down and take him away from them by force, and bring him into the barracks" (Ac. 23:6-10).

An Angel of the God to Whom I Belong

"When they had gone a long time without food, then Paul stood up in their midst and said, 'Men, you ought to have followed my advice and not to have set sail from Crete and incurred this damage and loss. Yet now I urge you to keep up your courage, for there will be no loss of life among you, but only of the ship. For this very night an angel of the God to whom I belong and whom I serve stood before me, saying, "Do not be afraid, Paul; you must stand before Caesar; and behold, God has granted you all those who are sailing with you." Therefore, keep up your courage, men, for I believe God that it will turn out exactly as I have been told. But we must run aground on a certain island'" (Ac. 27:21-26).

Even Satan Disguises Himself as an Angel of Light

"But what I am doing I will continue to do, so that I may cut off opportunity from those who desire an opportunity to be regarded just as we are in the matter about which they are boasting. For such men are false apostles, deceitful workers, disguising themselves as apostles of Christ. No wonder, for even Satan disguises himself as an angel of light. Therefore it is not surprising if his servants also disguise themselves as servants of righteousness, whose end will be according to their deeds" (2Co. 11:12-15).

If We, or an Angel from Heaven

"I am amazed that you are so quickly deserting Him who called you by the grace of Christ, for a different gospel; which is really not another; only there are some who are disturbing you and want to distort the gospel of Christ. But even if we, or an angel from heaven, should preach to you a gospel contrary to what we have preached to you, he is to be accursed! As we have said before, so I say again now, if any man is preaching to you a gospel contrary to what you received, he is to be accursed" (Gal. 1:6-9)!

You Received Me as an Angel of God, as Christ Jesus Himself

"I beg of you, brethren, become as I am, for I also have become as you are. You have done me no wrong; but you know that it was because of a bodily illness that I preached the gospel to you the first time; and that which was a trial to you in my bodily condition you did not despise or loathe, but you received me as an angel of God, as Christ Jesus Himself. Where then is that sense of blessing you had? For I bear you witness that, if possible, you would have plucked out your eyes and given them to me. So have I become your enemy by telling you the truth? They eagerly seek you, not commendably, but they wish to shut you out so that you will seek them. But it is good always to be eagerly sought in a commendable manner, and not only when I am present with you. My children, with whom I am again in labor until Christ is formed in you—but I could wish to be present with you now and to change my tone, for I am perplexed about you" (Gal. 4:12-20).

He Sent and Communicated It by His Angel to His Bond-Servant John

"The Revelation of Jesus Christ, which God gave Him to show to His bond-servants, the things which must soon take place; and He sent and communicated it by His angel to His bond-servant John, who testified to the word of God and to the testimony of Jesus Christ, even to all that he saw. Blessed is he who reads and those who hear the words of the prophecy, and heed the things which are written in it; for the time is near" (Rev. 1:1-3).

The Angel of the Church in Ephesus

"To the angel of the church in Ephesus write: The One who holds the seven stars in His right hand, the One who walks among the seven golden lampstands, says this: 'I know your deeds and your toil and perseverance, and that you cannot tolerate evil men, and you put to the test those who call themselves apostles, and they are not, and you found them to be false; and you have perseverance and have endured for My name's sake, and have not grown weary. But I have this against you, that you have left your first love. Therefore remember from where you have fallen, and repent and do the deeds you did at first; or else I am coming to you and will remove your lampstand out of its place—unless you repent. Yet this you do have, that you hate the deeds of the Nicolaitans, which I also hate. He who has an ear, let him hear what the Spirit says to the churches. To him who overcomes, I will grant to eat of the tree of life which is in the Paradise of God'" (Rev. 2:1-7).

The Angel of the Church in Smyrna

"And to the angel of the church in Smyrna write: The first and the last, who was dead, and has come to life, says this: I know your tribulation and your poverty (but you are rich), and the blasphemy by those who say they are Jews and are not, but are a synagogue of Satan. Do not fear what you are about to suffer. Behold, the devil is about to cast some of you into prison, so that you will be tested, and you will have tribulation for ten days. Be faithful until death, and I will give you the crown of life. He who has an ear, let him hear what the

Spirit says to the churches. He who overcomes will not be hurt by the second death" (Rev. 2:8-11).

The Angel of the Church in Pergamum

"And to the angel of the church in Pergamum write: The One who has the sharp two-edged sword says this: I know where you dwell, where Satan's throne is; and you hold fast My name, and did not deny My faith even in the days of Antipas, My witness, My faithful one, who was killed among you, where Satan dwells. But I have a few things against you, because you have there some who hold the teaching of Balaam, who kept teaching Balak to put a stumbling block before the sons of Israel, to eat things sacrificed to idols and to commit acts of immorality. So you also have some who in the same way hold the teaching of the Nicolaitans. Therefore repent; or else I am coming to you quickly, and I will make war against them with the sword of My mouth. He who has an ear, let him hear what the Spirit says to the churches. To him who overcomes, to him I will give some of the hidden manna, and I will give him a white stone, and a new name written on the stone which no one knows but he who receives it" (Rev. 2:12-17).

The Angel of the Church in Thyatira

"And to the angel of the church in Thyatira write: The Son of God, who has eyes like a flame of fire, and His feet are like burnished bronze, says this: I know your deeds, and your love and faith and service and perseverance, and that your deeds of late are greater than at first. But I have this against you, that you tolerate the woman Jezebel, who calls herself a prophetess, and she teaches and leads My bond-servants astray so that they commit acts of immorality and eat things sacrificed to idols. I gave her time to repent, and she does not want to repent of her immorality. Behold, I will throw her on a bed of sickness, and those who commit adultery with her into great tribulation, unless they repent of her deeds. And I will kill her children with pestilence, and all the churches will know that I am He who searches the minds and hearts; and I will give to each one of you according to your deeds. But I say to you, the rest who are in Thyatira, who do not hold this teaching, who have not known the deep things of Satan, as they call them—I place no other burden on you. Nevertheless what you have, hold fast until I come. He who overcomes, and he who keeps My deeds until the end, TO HIM I WILL GIVE AUTHORITY OVER THE NATIONS; AND HE SHALL RULE THEM WITH A ROD OF IRON, AS THE VESSELS OF THE POTTER ARE BROKEN TO PIECES, as I also have received authority from My Father; and I will give him the morning star. He who has an ear, let him hear what the Spirit says to the churches" (Rev. 2:18-29).

The Angel of the Church in Sardis

"To the angel of the church in Sardis write: He who has the seven Spirits of God and the seven stars, says this: 'I know your deeds, that you have a name that you are alive, but you are dead. Wake up, and strengthen the things that remain, which were about to die; for I have not found your deeds completed in the sight of My God. So remember what you have received and heard; and keep it, and repent. Therefore if you do not wake up, I will come like a thief, and you will not know at what hour I will come to you. But you have a few people in Sardis who have not soiled their garments; and they will walk with Me in white, for they are worthy. He who overcomes will thus be clothed in white garments; and I will not erase his name from the book of life, and I will confess his name before My Father and before His angels. He who has an ear, let him hear what the Spirit says to the churches'" (Rev. 3:1-6).

The Angel of the Church in Philadelphia

"And to the angel of the church in Philadelphia write: He who is holy, who is true, who has the key of David, who opens and no one will shut, and who shuts and no one opens, says this: I know your deeds. Behold, I have put before you an open door which no one can shut, because you have a little power, and have kept My word, and have not denied My name. Behold, I will cause those of the synagogue of Satan, who say that they are Jews and are not, but lie—I will make them come and bow down at your feet, and make them know that I have loved you. Because you have kept the word of My perseverance, I also will keep you from the hour of testing, that hour which is about to come upon the whole world, to test those who dwell on the earth. I am coming quickly; hold fast what you have, so that no one will take your crown. He who overcomes, I will make him a pillar in the temple of My God, and he will not go out from it anymore; and I will write on him the name of My God, and the name of the city of My God, the new Jerusalem, which comes down out of heaven from My God, and My new name. He who has an ear, let him hear what the Spirit says to the churches" (Rev. 3:7-13).

The Angel of the Church in Laodicea

"To the angel of the church in Laodicea write: The Amen, the faithful and true Witness, the Beginning of the creation of God, says this: I know your deeds, that you are neither cold nor hot; I wish that you were cold or hot. So because you are lukewarm, and neither hot nor cold, I will spit you out of My mouth. Because you say, 'I am rich, and have become wealthy, and have need of nothing,' and you do not know that you are wretched and miserable and poor and blind and naked, I advise you to buy from Me gold refined by fire so that you may become rich, and white garments so that you may clothe yourself, and that the shame of your nakedness will not be revealed; and eye salve to anoint your eyes so that you may see. Those whom I love, I reprove and discipline; therefore be zealous and repent. Behold, I stand at the door and knock; if anyone hears My voice and opens the door, I will come in to him and will dine with him, and he with Me. He who overcomes, I will grant to him to sit down with Me on My throne, as I also overcame and sat down with My Father on His throne. He who has an ear, let him hear what the Spirit says to the churches" (Rev. 3:14-22).

I Saw a Strong Angel Proclaiming

"I saw in the right hand of Him who sat on the throne a book written inside and on the back, sealed up with seven seals. And I saw a strong angel proclaiming with a loud voice, 'Who is worthy to open the book and to break its seals?' And no one in heaven or on the earth or under the earth was able to open the book or to look into it. Then I began to weep greatly because no one was found worthy to open the book or to look into it; and one of the elders said to me, 'Stop weeping; behold, the Lion that is from the tribe of Judah, the Root of David, has overcome so as to open the book and its seven seals'" (Rev. 5:1-5).

I Saw Another Angel Ascending from the Rising of the Sun

"After this I saw four angels standing at the four corners of the earth, holding back the four winds of the earth, so that no wind would blow on the earth or on the sea or on any tree. And I saw another angel ascending from the rising of the sun, having the seal of the living God; and he cried out with a loud voice to the four angels to whom it was granted to harm the earth and the sea, saying, 'Do not harm the earth or the sea or the trees until we have sealed the bond-servants of our God on their foreheads'" (Rev. 7:1-3).

Prayers of the Saints, Went Up Before God Out of the Angel's Hand

"Another angel came and stood at the altar, holding a golden censer; and much incense was given to him, so that he might add it to the prayers of all the saints on the golden altar which was before the throne. And the smoke of the incense, with the prayers of the saints, went up before God out of the angel's hand. Then the angel took the censer and filled it with the fire of the altar, and threw it to the earth; and there followed peals of thunder and sounds and flashes of lightning and an earthquake" (Rev. 8:3-5).

The Second Angel Sounded

"The second angel sounded, and something like a great mountain burning with fire was thrown into the sea; and a third of the sea became blood, and a third of the creatures which were in the sea and had life, died; and a third of the ships were destroyed" (Rev. 8:8-9).

The Third Angel Sounded

"The third angel sounded, and a great star fell from heaven, burning like a torch, and it fell on a third of the rivers and on the springs of waters. The name of the star is called Wormwood; and a third of the waters became wormwood, and many men died from the waters, because they were made bitter" (Rev. 8:10-11).

The Fourth Angel Sounded

"The fourth angel sounded, and a third of the sun and a third of the moon and a third of the stars were struck, so that a third of them would be darkened and the day would not shine for a third of it, and the night in the same way" (Rev. 8:12).

The Fifth Angel Sounded

"Then the fifth angel sounded, and I saw a star from heaven which had fallen to the earth; and the key of the bottomless pit was given to him. He opened the bottomless pit, and smoke went up out of the pit, like the smoke of a great furnace; and the sun and the air were darkened by the smoke of the pit. Then out of the smoke came locusts upon the earth, and power was given them, as the scorpions of the earth have power. They were told not to hurt the grass of the earth, nor any green thing, nor any tree, but only the men who do not have the seal of God on their foreheads. And they were not permitted to kill anyone, but to torment for five months; and their torment was like the torment of a scorpion when it stings a man. And in those days men will seek death and will not find it; they will long to die, and death flees from them" (Rev. 9:1-6).

The Angel of the Abyss

"The appearance of the locusts was like horses prepared for battle; and on their heads appeared to be crowns like gold, and their faces were like the faces of men. They had hair like the hair of women, and their teeth were like the teeth of lions. They had breastplates like breastplates of iron; and the sound of their wings was like the sound of chariots, of many horses rushing to battle. They have tails like scorpions, and stings; and in their tails is their power to hurt men for five months. They have as king over them, the angel of the abyss; his name in Hebrew is Abaddon, and in the Greek he has the name Apollyon" (Rev. 9:7-11).

The Sixth Angel Sounded

"Then the sixth angel sounded, and I heard a voice from the four horns of the golden altar which is before God, one saying to the sixth angel who had the trumpet, 'Release the four angels who are bound at the great river Euphrates.' And the four angels, who had been prepared for the hour and day and month and year, were released, so that they would kill a third of mankind. The number of the armies of the horsemen was two hundred million; I heard the number of them. And this is how I saw in the vision the horses and those who sat on them: the riders had breastplates the color of fire and of hyacinth and of brimstone; and the heads of the horses are like the heads of lions; and out of their mouths proceed fire and smoke and brimstone. A third of mankind was killed by these three plagues, by the fire and the smoke and the brimstone which proceeded out of their mouths. For the power of the horses is in their mouths and in their tails; for their tails are like serpents and have heads, and with them they do harm" (Rev. 9:13-19).

I Saw Another Strong Angel and His Face Was Like the Sun

"I saw another strong angel coming down out of heaven, clothed with a cloud; and the rainbow was upon his head, and his face was like the sun, and his feet like pillars of fire; and he had in his hand a little book which was open. He placed his right foot on the sea and his left on the land; and he cried out with a loud voice, as when a lion roars; and when he had cried out, the seven peals of thunder uttered their voices. When the seven peals of thunder had spoken, I was about to write; and I heard a voice from heaven saying, 'Seal up the things which the seven peals of thunder have spoken and do not write them.' Then the angel whom I saw standing on the sea and on the land lifted up his right hand to heaven, and swore by Him who lives forever and ever, WHO CREATED HEAVEN AND THE

THINGS IN IT, AND THE EARTH AND THE THINGS IN IT, AND THE SEA AND THE THINGS IN IT, that there will be delay no longer, but in the days of the voice of the seventh angel, when he is about to sound, then the mystery of God is finished, as He preached to His servants the prophets" (Rev. 10:1-7).

Go, Take the Book Which Is Open in the Hand of the Angel

"Then the voice which I heard from heaven, I heard again speaking with me, and saying, 'Go, take the book which is open in the hand of the angel who stands on the sea and on the land.' So I went to the angel, telling him to give me the little book. And he said to me, 'Take it and eat it; it will make your stomach bitter, but in your mouth it will be sweet as honey.' I took the little book out of the angel's hand and ate it, and in my mouth it was sweet as honey; and when I had eaten it, my stomach was made bitter. And they said to me, 'You must prophesy again concerning many peoples and nations and tongues and kings'" (Rev. 10:8-11).

The Seventh Angel Sounded

"Then the seventh angel sounded; and there were loud voices in heaven, saying, 'The kingdom of the world has become the kingdom of our Lord and of His Christ; and He will reign forever and ever.' And the twenty-four elders, who sit on their thrones before God, fell on their faces and worshiped God, saying, 'We give You thanks, O Lord God, the Almighty, who are and who were, because You have taken Your great power and have begun to reign. And the nations were enraged, and Your wrath came, and the time came for the dead to be judged, and the time to reward Your bond-servants the prophets and the saints and those who fear Your name, the small and the great, and to destroy those who destroy the earth'" (Rev. 11:15-18).

An Angel in Midheaven

"And I saw another angel flying in midheaven, having an eternal gospel to preach to those who live on the earth, and to every nation and tribe and tongue and people; and he said with a loud voice, 'Fear God, and give Him glory, because the hour of His judgment has come; worship Him who made the heaven and the earth and sea and springs of waters'" (Rev. 14:6-7).

Another Angel

"And another angel, a second one, followed, saying, 'Fallen, fallen is Babylon the great, she who has made all the nations drink of the wine of the passion of her immorality'" (Rev. 14:8).

An Angel with a Loud Voice

"Then another angel, a third one, followed them, saying with a loud voice, 'If anyone worships the beast and his image, and receives a mark on his forehead or on his hand, he also will drink of the wine of the wrath of God, which is mixed in full strength in the cup of His anger; and he will be tormented with fire and brimstone in the presence of the holy angels and in the presence of the Lamb. And the smoke of their torment goes up forever and ever; they have no rest day and night, those who worship the beast and his image, and whoever receives the mark of his name.' Here is the perseverance of the saints who keep the commandments of God and their faith in Jesus" (Rev. 14:9-12).

Another Angel Came Out of the Temple, Crying Out

"Then I looked, and behold, a white cloud, and sitting on the cloud was one like a son of man, having a golden crown on His head and a sharp sickle in His hand. And another angel came out of the temple, crying out with a loud voice to Him who sat on the cloud, 'Put in your sickle and reap, for the hour to reap has come, because the harvest of the earth is ripe.' Then He who sat on the cloud swung His sickle over the earth, and the earth was reaped" (Rev. 14:14-16).

An Angel with a Sharp Sickle

"And another angel came out of the temple which is in heaven, and he also had a sharp sickle. Then another angel, the one who has power over fire, came out from the altar; and he called with a loud voice to him who had the sharp sickle, saying, 'Put in your sharp sickle and gather the clusters from the vine of the earth, because her grapes are ripe.' So the angel swung his sickle to the earth and gathered the clusters from the vine of the earth, and threw them into the great wine press of the wrath of God. And the wine press was trodden outside the city, and blood came out from the wine press, up to the horses' bridles, for a distance of two hundred miles" (Rev. 14:17-20).

Chapter Four

I Heard the Angel

"Then the third angel poured out his bowl into the rivers and the springs of waters; and they became blood. And I heard the angel of the waters saying, 'Righteous are You, who are and who were, O Holy One, because You judged these things; for they poured out the blood of saints and prophets, and You have given them blood to drink. They deserve it.' And I heard the altar saying, 'Yes, O Lord God, the Almighty, true and righteous are Your judgments'" (Rev. 16:4-7).

The Angel Poured

"The fourth angel poured out his bowl upon the sun, and it was given to it to scorch men with fire. Men were scorched with fierce heat; and they blasphemed the name of God who has the power over these plagues, and they did not repent so as to give Him glory. Then the fifth angel poured out his bowl on the throne of the beast, and his kingdom became darkened; and they gnawed their tongues because of pain, and they blasphemed the God of heaven because of their pains and their sores; and they did not repent of their deeds. The sixth angel poured out his bowl on the great river, the Euphrates; and its water was dried up, so that the way would be prepared for the kings from the east" (Rev. 16:8-12).

The Seventh Angel Poured

"Then the seventh angel poured out his bowl upon the air, and a loud voice came out of the temple from the throne, saying, 'It is done.' And there were flashes of lightning and sounds and peals of thunder; and there was a great earthquake, such as there had not been since man came to be upon the earth, so great an earthquake was it, and so mighty. The great city was split into three parts, and the cities of the nations fell. Babylon the great was remembered before God, to give her the cup of the wine of His fierce wrath. And every island fled away, and the mountains were not found. And huge hailstones, about one hundred pounds each, came down from heaven upon men; and men blasphemed God because of the plague of the hail, because its plague *was extremely severe" (Rev. 16:17-21).

The Angel Said to Me

"Then one of the seven angels who had the seven bowls came and spoke with me, saying, 'Come here, I will show you the judgment of the great harlot who sits on many waters, with whom the kings of the earth committed acts of immorality, and those who dwell on the earth were made drunk with the wine of her immorality.' And he carried me away in the Spirit into a wilderness; and I saw a woman sitting on a scarlet beast, full of blasphemous names, having seven heads and ten horns. The woman was clothed in purple and scarlet, and adorned with gold and precious stones and pearls, having in her hand a gold cup full of abominations and of the unclean things of her immorality, and on her forehead a name was written, a mystery, 'BABYLON THE GREAT, THE MOTHER OF HARLOTS AND OF THE ABOMINATIONS OF THE EARTH.' And I saw the woman drunk with the blood of the saints, and with the blood of the witnesses of Jesus. When I saw her, I wondered greatly. And the angel said to me, 'Why do you wonder? I will tell you the mystery of the woman and of the beast that carries her, which has the seven heads and the ten horns'" (Rev. 17:1-7).

I Saw an Angel Having Great Authority

"After these things I saw another angel coming down from heaven, having great authority, and the earth was illumined with his glory. And he cried out with a mighty voice, saying, 'Fallen, fallen is Babylon the great! She has become a dwelling place of demons and a prison of every unclean spirit, and a prison of every unclean and hateful bird. For all the nations have drunk of the wine of the passion of her immorality, and the kings of the earth have committed acts of immorality with her, and the merchants of the earth have become rich by the wealth of her sensuality'" (Rev. 18:1-3).

A Strong Angel

"Then a strong angel took up a stone like a great millstone and threw it into the sea, saying, 'So will Babylon, the great city, be thrown down with violence, and will not be found any longer. And the sound of harpists and musicians and flute-players and trumpeters will not be heard in you any longer; and no craftsman of any craft will be found in you any longer; and the sound of a mill will not be heard in you any longer; and the light of a lamp will not shine in you any longer; and the voice of the bridegroom and bride will not be heard in you any longer; for your merchants were the great men of the earth, because all the nations were deceived by your sorcery. And in her was found the blood of prophets and of saints and of all who have been slain on the earth'" (Rev. 18:21-24).

I Saw an Angel Standing in the Sun

"Then I saw an angel standing in the sun, and he cried out with a loud voice, saying to all the birds which fly in midheaven, 'Come, assemble for the great supper of God, so that you may eat the flesh of kings and the flesh of commanders and the flesh of mighty men and the flesh of horses and of those who sit on them and the flesh of all men, both free men and slaves, and small and great'" (Rev. 19:17-18).

I Saw an Angel Holding a Key

"Then I saw an angel coming down from heaven, holding the key of the abyss and a great chain in his hand. And he laid hold of the dragon, the serpent of old, who is the devil and Satan, and bound him for a thousand years; and he threw him into the abyss, and shut it and sealed it over him, so that he would not deceive the nations any longer, until the thousand years were completed; after these things he must be released for a short time" (Rev. 20:1-3).

The Lord Sent His Angel to Show to His Bond-servants the Things Which Must Soon Take Place

"And he said to me, 'These words are faithful and true'; and the Lord, the God of the spirits of the prophets, sent His angel to show to His bond-servants the things which must soon take place. 'And behold, I am coming quickly. Blessed is he who heeds the words of the prophecy of this book.' I, John, am the one who heard and saw these things. And when I heard and saw, I fell down to worship at the feet of the angel who showed me these things. But he said to me, 'Do not do that. I am a fellow servant of yours and of your brethren the prophets and of those who heed the words of this book. Worship God'" (Rev. 22:6-9).

I, Jesus, Have Sent My Angel to Testify

"I, Jesus, have sent My angel to testify to you these things for the churches. I am the root and the descendant of David, the bright morning star" (Rev. 22:16).

Chapter Five

ANGELS IN THE NEW TESTAMENT

He Will Command His Angels Concerning You

"Then the devil took Him into the holy city; and he had Him stand on the pinnacle of the temple, and said to Him, 'If You are the Son of God throw Yourself down; for it is written, "HE WILL GIVE HIS ANGELS CHARGE CONCERNING YOU"; and "ON their HANDS THEY WILL BEAR YOU UP, LEST YOU STRIKE YOUR FOOT AGAINST A STONE.'" Jesus said to him, 'On the other hand, it is written, "YOU SHALL NOT PUT THE LORD YOUR GOD TO THE TEST.'"" (Mt. 4:5-7).

Behold, Angels Came and Began to Minister to Him

"Again, the devil took Him to a very high mountain, and showed Him all the kingdoms of the world, and their glory; and he said to Him, 'All these things will I give You, if You fall down and worship me.' Then Jesus said to him, 'Begone, Satan! For it is written, "YOU SHALL WORSHIP THE LORD YOUR GOD, AND SERVE HIM ONLY.'" Then the devil left Him; and behold, angels came and began to minister to Him" (Mt. 4:8-11).

The Reapers Are Angels

"Then He left the multitudes, and went into the house. And His disciples came to Him, saying, 'Explain to us the parable of the tares of the field.' And He answered and said, 'The one who sows the good seed is the Son of Man, and the field is the world; and as for the good seed, these are the sons of the kingdom; and the tares are the sons of the evil one; and the enemy who sowed them is the devil, and the harvest is the end of the age; and the reapers are angels. Therefore just as the tares are gathered up and burned with fire, so shall it be at the end of the age. The Son of Man will send forth His angels, and they will gather out of His kingdom all stumbling blocks, and those who commit lawlessness, and will cast them into the furnace of fire; in that place there shall be weeping and gnashing of teeth. Then THE RIGHTEOUS WILL SHINE FORTH AS THE SUN in the kingdom of their Father. He who has ears, let him hear'" (Mt. 13:36-43).

The Angels Will Come Forth and Take out the Wicked

"Again, the kingdom of heaven is like a dragnet cast into the sea, and gathering fish of every kind; and when it was filled, they drew it up on the beach; and they sat down, and gathered the good fish into containers, but the bad they threw away. So it will be at the end of the age; the angels shall come forth, and take out the wicked from among the righteous, and will cast them into the furnace of fire; there shall be weeping and gnashing of teeth" (Mt. 13:47-50).

In the Glory of His Father with His Angels

"Then Jesus said to His disciples, 'If anyone wishes to come after Me, let him deny himself, and take up his cross, and follow Me. For whoever wishes to save his life shall lose it; but whoever loses his life for My sake shall find it. For what will a man be profited, if he gains the whole world, and forfeits his soul? Or what will a man give in exchange for his soul? For the Son of Man is going to come in the glory of His Father with His angels; and WILL THEN RECOMPENSE EVERY MAN ACCORDING TO HIS DEEDS'" (Mt. 16:24-27).

Chapter Five

Their Angels in Heaven

"See that you do not despise one of these little ones, for I say to you, that their angels in heaven continually behold the face of My Father who is in heaven. For the Son of Man has come to save that which was lost" (Mt. 18:10-11).

Neither Marry nor Are Given in Marriage, but Are Like Angels in Heaven

"But Jesus answered and said to them, 'You are mistaken, not understanding the Scriptures, or the power of God. For in the resurrection they neither marry, nor are given in marriage, but are like angels in heaven. But regarding the resurrection of the dead, have you not read that which was spoken to you by God, saying, "I AM THE GOD OF ABRAHAM, AND THE GOD OF ISAAC, AND THE GOD OF JACOB"? He is not the God of the dead but of the living.' And when the multitudes heard this, they were astonished at His teaching" (Mt. 22:29-33).

Are Like Angels in Heaven

"But immediately after the tribulation of those days THE SUN WILL BE DARKENED, AND THE MOON WILL NOT GIVE ITS LIGHT, AND THE STARS WILL FALL from the sky, and the powers of the heavens will be shaken, and then the sign of the Son of Man will appear in the sky, and then all the tribes of the earth will mourn, and they will see the SON OF MAN COMING ON THE CLOUDS OF THE SKY with power and great glory. And He will send forth His angels with A GREAT TRUMPET and THEY WILL GATHER TOGETHER His elect from the four winds, from one end of the sky to the other" (Mt.

24:29-31).

Not Even the Angels of Heaven

"But of that day and hour no one knows, not even the angels of heaven, nor the Son, but the Father alone. For the coming of the Son of Man will be just like the days of Noah. For as in those days which were before the flood they were eating and drinking, they were marrying and giving in marriage, until the day that Noah entered the ark, and they did not understand until the flood came and took them all away; so shall the coming of the Son of Man be. Then there shall be two men in the field; one will be taken, and one will be left. Two women will be grinding at the mill; one will be taken, and one will be left" (Mt. 24:36-41).

In His Glory, and All the Angels with Him

"But when the Son of Man comes in His glory, and all the angels with Him, then He will sit on His glorious throne. And all the nations will be gathered before Him; and He will separate them from one another, as the shepherd separates the sheep from the goats; and He will put the sheep on His right, and the goats on the left" (Mt. 25:31-33).

Twelve Legions of Angels

"And behold, one of those who were with Jesus reached and drew out his sword, and struck the slave of the high priest, and cut off his ear. Then Jesus said to him, 'Put your sword back into its place; for all those who take up the sword shall perish by the sword. Or do you think that I cannot appeal to My Father, and He will at once put at My disposal more than twelve legions of angels? How then shall the Scriptures be fulfilled, that it must happen this way?'" (Mt. 26:51-54).

The Angels Were Ministering

"And immediately the Spirit impelled Him to go out into the wilderness. And He was in the wilderness forty days being tempted by Satan; and He was with the wild beasts, and the angels were ministering to Him" (Mk. 1:12-13).

The Glory of His Father with the Holy Angels

"And He summoned the multitude with His disciples, and said to them, 'If anyone wishes to come after Me, let him deny himself, and take up his cross, and follow Me. For whoever wishes to save his life shall lose it; but whoever loses his life for My sake and the gospel's shall save it. For what does it profit a man to gain the whole world, and forfeit his soul? For what shall a man give in exchange for his soul? For whoever is ashamed of Me and My words in this adulterous and sinful generation, the Son of Man will also be ashamed of him when He comes in the glory of His Father with the holy angels'" (Mk. 8:34-38).

Angels in Heaven

"And some Sadducees (who say that there is no resurrection) came to Him, and began questioning Him, saying, 'Teacher, Moses wrote for us that IF A MAN'S BROTHER DIES, and leaves behind a wife, AND LEAVES NO CHILD, HIS BROTHER SHOULD TAKE THE WIFE, AND RAISE UP OFFSPRING TO HIS BROTHER. There were seven brothers; and the first took a wife, and died, leaving no offspring. And the second one took her, and died, leaving behind no offspring; and the third likewise; and so all seven left no offspring. Last of all the woman died also. In the resurrection, when they rise again, which one's wife will she be? For all seven had her as wife.' Jesus said to them, 'Is this not the reason you are mistaken, that you do not understand the Scriptures, or the power of God? For when they rise from the dead, they neither marry, nor are given in marriage, but are like angels in heaven. But regarding the fact that the dead rise again, have you not read in the book of Moses, in the passage about the burning bush, how God spoke to him, saying, "I AM THE GOD OF ABRAHAM, AND THE GOD OF ISAAC, AND THE GOD OF JACOB"? He is not the God of the dead, but of the living; you are greatly mistaken'" (Mk. 12:18-27).

He Will Send Forth the Angels, and Will Gather Together His Elect

"But in those days, after that tribulation, THE SUN WILL BE DARKENED, AND THE MOON WILL NOT GIVE ITS LIGHT, AND THE STARS WILL BE FALLING from heaven, and the powers that are in the heavens will be shaken. And then they will see THE SON OF MAN COMING IN CLOUDS with great power and glory. And then He will send forth the angels, and will gather together His elect from the four winds, from the farthest end of the earth, to the farthest end of heaven" (Mk. 13:24-27).

No One Knows, Not Even the Angels in Heaven

"Now learn the parable from the fig tree: when its branch has already become tender, and puts forth its leaves, you know that summer is near. Even so, you too, when you see these things happening, recognize that He is near, right at the door. Truly I say to you, this generation will not pass away until all these things take place. Heaven and earth will pass away, but My words will not pass away. But of that day or hour no one knows, not even the angels in heaven, nor the Son, but the Father alone" (Mk. 13:28-32).

The Angels Had Gone Away

"And it came about when the angels had gone away from them into heaven, that the shepherds began saying to one another, 'Let us go straight to Bethlehem then, and see this thing that has happened which the Lord has made known to us.' And they came in haste and found their way to Mary and Joseph, and the baby as He lay in the manger. And when they had seen this, they made known the statement which had been told them about this Child. And all who heard it wondered at the things which were told them by the shepherds. But Mary treasured up all these things, pondering them in her heart. And the shepherds went back, glorifying and praising God for all that they had heard and seen, just as had been told them" (Lk. 2:15-20).

He Will Command His Angels to Guard You

"And he led Him to Jerusalem and had Him stand on the pinnacle of the temple, and said to Him, 'If You are the Son of God, throw Yourself down from here; for it is written, "HE WILL GIVE HIS ANGELS CHARGE CONCERNING YOU TO GUARD YOU," and, "ON their HANDS THEY WILL BEAR YOU UP, LEST YOU STRIKE YOUR FOOT AGAINST A STONE.'" And Jesus answered and said to him, 'It is said, "YOU SHALL NOT PUT THE

LORD YOUR GOD TO THE TEST"'"" (Lk. 4:9-12).

The Glory of the Father and of the Holy Angels

"And He was saying to them all, 'If anyone wishes to come after Me, let him deny himself, and take up his cross daily, and follow Me. For whoever wishes to save his life shall lose it, but whoever loses his life for My sake, he is the one who will save it. For what is a man profited if he gains the whole world, and loses or forfeits himself? For whoever is ashamed of Me and My words, of him will the Son of Man be ashamed when He comes in His glory, and the glory of the Father and of the holy angels. But I say to you truthfully, there are some of those standing here who shall not taste death until they see the kingdom of God'" (Lk. 9:23-27).

Denied Before the Angels of God

"And I say to you, everyone who confesses Me before men, the Son of Man shall confess him also before the angels of God; but he who denies Me before men shall be denied before the angels of God. And everyone who will speak a word against the Son of Man, it shall be forgiven him; but he who blasphemes against the Holy Spirit, it shall not be forgiven him. And when they bring you before the synagogues and the rulers and the authorities, do not become anxious about how or what you should speak in your defense, or what you should say; for the Holy Spirit will teach you in that very hour what you ought to say" (Lk. 12:8-12).

Chapter Five

There Is Joy in the Presence of the Angels

"Or what woman, if she has ten silver coins and loses one coin, does not light a lamp and sweep the house and search carefully until she finds it? And when she has found it, she calls together her friends and neighbors, saying, 'Rejoice with me, for I have found the coin which I had lost!' In the same way, I tell you, there is joy in the presence of the angels of God over one sinner who repents" (Lk. 15:8-10).

The Poor Man Died and Was Carried Away by the Angels

"Now there was a certain rich man, and he habitually dressed in purple and fine linen, gaily living in splendor every day. And a certain poor man named Lazarus was laid at his gate, covered with sores, and longing to be fed with the crumbs which were falling from the rich man's table; besides, even the dogs were coming and licking his sores. Now it came about that the poor man died and he was carried away by the angels to Abraham's bosom; and the rich man also died and was buried. And in Hades he lifted up his eyes, being in torment, and saw Abraham far away, and Lazarus in his bosom. And he cried out and said, 'Father Abraham, have mercy on me, and send Lazarus, that he may dip the tip of his finger in water and cool off my tongue; for I am in agony in this flame.' But Abraham said, 'Child, remember that during your life you received your good things, and likewise Lazarus bad things; but now he is being comforted here, and you are in agony. And besides all this, between us and you there is a great chasm fixed, in order that those who wish to come over from here to you may not be able, and that none may cross over from there to us.' And he said,

'Then I beg you, Father, that you send him to my father's house—for I have five brothers—that he may warn them, lest they also come to this place of torment.' But Abraham said, 'They have Moses and the Prophets; let them hear them.' But he said, 'No, Father Abraham, but if someone goes to them from the dead, they will repent!' But he said to him, 'If they do not listen to Moses and the Prophets, neither will they be persuaded if someone rises from the dead'" (Lk. 16:19-31).

Like Angels

"And Jesus said to them, 'The sons of this age marry and are given in marriage, but those who are considered worthy to attain to that age and the resurrection from the dead, neither marry, nor are given in marriage; for neither can they die anymore, for they are like angels, and are sons of God, being sons of the resurrection. But that the dead are raised, even Moses showed, in the passage about the burning bush, where he calls the Lord THE GOD OF ABRAHAM, AND THE GOD OF ISAAC, AND THE GOD OF JACOB. Now He is not the God of the dead, but of the living; for all live to Him.' And some of the scribes answered and said, 'Teacher, You have spoken well.' For they did not have courage to question Him any longer about anything" (Lk. 20:34-40).

They Had Also Seen a Vision of Angels

"And behold, two of them were going that very day to a village named Emmaus, which was about seven miles from Jerusalem. And they were conversing with each other about all these things which had taken place. And it came about that while they were conversing and discussing, Jesus Himself approached, and began traveling with them. But their eyes were prevented from recognizing Him. And He said to them, 'What are these words that you are exchanging with one another as you are walking?' And they stood still, looking sad. And one of them, named Cleopas, answered and said to Him, 'Are You the only one visiting Jerusalem and unaware of the things which have happened here in these days?' And He said to them, 'What things?' And they said to Him, 'The things about Jesus the Nazarene, who was a prophet mighty in deed and word in the sight of God and all the people, and how the chief priests and our rulers delivered Him up to the sentence of death, and crucified Him. But we were hoping that it was He who was going to redeem Israel. Indeed, besides all this, it is the third day since these things happened. But also some women among us amazed us. When they were at the tomb early in the morning, and did not find His body, they came, saying that they had also seen a vision of angels, who said that He was alive. And some of those who were with us went to the tomb and found it just exactly as the women also had said; but Him they did not see.' And He said to them, 'O foolish men and slow of heart to believe in all that the prophets have spoken! Was it not necessary for the Christ to suffer these things and to enter into His glory?' And beginning with Moses and with all the prophets, He explained to them the things concerning Himself in all the Scriptures" (Lk. 24:13-27).

You Will See the Heavens Opened and the Angels of God Ascending and Descending on the Son of Man

"The next day He purposed to go forth into Galilee, and He *found Philip. And Jesus said to him, 'Follow Me.' Now Philip was from Bethsaida, of the city of Andrew and Peter. Philip found Nathanael and said to him, 'We have found Him of whom Moses in the Law and also the Prophets wrote, Jesus of Nazareth, the son of Joseph.' And Nathanael said to him, 'Can any good thing come out of Nazareth?' Philip said to him, 'Come and see.' Jesus saw Nathanael coming to Him, and said of him, 'Behold, an Israelite indeed, in whom is no guile!' Nathanael said to Him, 'How do You know me?' Jesus answered and said to him, 'Before Philip called you, when you were under the fig tree, I saw you.' Nathanael answered Him, 'Rabbi, You are the Son of God; You are the King of Israel.' Jesus answered and said to him, 'Because I said to you that I saw you under the fig tree, do you believe? You shall see greater things than these.' And He said to him, 'Truly, truly, I say to you, you shall see the heavens opened, and the angels of God ascending and descending on the Son of Man'" (Jn. 1:43-51).

She Saw Two Angels in White

"But Mary was standing outside the tomb weeping; and so, as she wept, she stooped and looked into the tomb; and she beheld two angels in white sitting, one at the head, and one at the feet, where the body of Jesus had been lying. And they said to her, 'Woman, why are you weeping?' She said to them, 'Because they have taken away my Lord, and I do not know where they have laid Him.' When she had said this, she turned around, and beheld Jesus standing there, and did not know that it was Jesus. Jesus said to her, 'Woman, why are you weeping? Whom are you seeking?' Supposing Him to be the gardener, she said to Him, 'Sir, if you have carried Him away, tell me where you have laid Him, and I will take Him away.' Jesus said to her, 'Mary!' She turned and said to Him in Hebrew, 'Rabboni!' (which means, Teacher). Jesus said to her, 'Stop clinging to Me, for I have not yet ascended to the Father; but go to My brethren, and say to them, "I ascend to My Father and your Father, and My God and your God.'" Mary Magdalene came, announcing to the disciples, 'I have seen the Lord,' and that He had said these things to her" (Jn. 20:11-18).

You Received the Law as Ordained by Angels

"You men who are stiff-necked and uncircumcised in heart and ears are always resisting the Holy Spirit; you are doing just as your fathers did. Which one of the prophets did your fathers not persecute? And they killed those who had previously announced the coming of the Righteous One, whose betrayers and murderers you have now become; you who received the law as ordained by angels, and yet did not keep it" (Ac. 7:51-53).

Neither Death, nor Life, nor Angels

"And in the same way the Spirit also helps our weakness; for we do not know how to pray as we should, but the Spirit Himself intercedes for us with groanings too deep for words; and He who searches the hearts knows what the mind of the Spirit is, because He intercedes for the saints according to the will of God. And we know that God causes all things to work together for good to those who love God, to those who are called according to His purpose. For whom He foreknew, He also predestined to become conformed to the image of His Son, that He might be the first-born among many brethren; and whom He predestined, these He also called; and whom He called, these He also justified; and whom He justified, these He also glorified. What then shall we say to these things? If God is for us, who is against us? He who did not spare His own Son, but delivered Him up for us all, how will He not also with Him freely give us all things? Who will bring a charge against God's elect? God is the one who justifies; who is the one who condemns? Christ Jesus is He who died, yes, rather who was raised, who is at the right hand of God, who also intercedes for us. Who shall separate us from the love of Christ? Shall tribulation, or distress, or persecution, or famine, or nakedness, or peril, or sword? Just as it is written, 'FOR THY SAKE WE ARE BEING PUT TO DEATH ALL DAY LONG; WE WERE CONSIDERED AS SHEEP TO BE SLAUGHTERED.' But in all these things we overwhelmingly conquer through Him who loved us. For I am convinced that neither death, nor life, nor angels, nor principalities, nor things present, nor things to come, nor powers, nor height, nor depth, nor any other created thing, shall be able to separate us from the love of God, which is in Christ Jesus our Lord" (Ro. 8:26-39).

Both to Angels and to Men

"You are already filled, you have already become rich, you have become kings without us; and I would indeed that you had become kings so that we also might reign with you. For, I think, God has exhibited us apostles last of all, as men condemned to death; because we have become a spectacle to the world, both to angels and to men. We are fools for Christ's sake, but you are prudent in Christ; we are weak, but you are strong; you are distinguished, but we are without honor. To this present hour we are both hungry and thirsty, and are poorly clothed, and are roughly treated, and are homeless; and we toil, working with our own hands; when we are reviled, we bless; when we are persecuted, we endure; when we are slandered, we try to conciliate; we have become as the scum of the world, the dregs of all things, even until now" (1Co. 4:8-13).

Do You Not Know that We Will Judge Angels

"Does any one of you, when he has a case against his neighbor, dare to go to law before the unrighteous, and not before the saints? Or do you not know that the saints will judge the world? And if the world is judged by you, are you not competent to constitute the smallest law courts? Do you not know that we shall judge angels? How much more, matters of this life? If then you have law courts dealing with matters of this life, do you appoint them as judges who are of no account in the church? I say this to your shame. Is it so, that there is not among you one wise man who will be able to decide between his brethren, but brother goes to law with brother, and that before unbelievers" (1Co. 6:1-6)?

Because of the Angels

"Now I praise you because you remember me in everything, and hold firmly to the traditions, just as I delivered them to you. But I want you to understand that Christ is the head of every man, and the man is the head of a woman, and God is the head of Christ. Every man who has something on his head while praying or prophesying, disgraces his head. But every woman who has her head uncovered while praying or prophesying, disgraces her head; for she is one and the same with her whose head is shaved. For if a woman does not cover her head, let her also have her hair cut off; but if it is disgraceful for a woman to have her hair cut off or her head shaved, let her cover her head. For a man ought not to have his head covered, since he is the image and glory of God; but the woman is the glory of man. For man does not originate from woman, but woman from man; for indeed man was not created for the woman's sake, but woman for the man's sake. Therefore the woman ought to have a symbol of authority on her head, because of the angels. However, in the Lord, neither is woman independent of man, nor is man independent of woman. For as the woman originates from the man, so also the man has his birth through the woman; and all things originate from God. Judge for yourselves: is it proper for a woman to pray to God with head uncovered? Does not even nature itself teach you that if a man has long hair, it is a dishonor to him, but if a woman has long hair, it is a glory to her? For her hair is given to her for a covering. But if one is inclined to be contentious, we have no other practice, nor have the churches of God" (1Co. 11:2-16).

And of Angels

"If I speak with the tongues of men and of angels, but do not have love, I have become a noisy gong or a clanging cymbal. And if I have the gift of prophecy, and know all mysteries and all knowledge; and if I have all faith, so as to remove mountains, but do not have love, I am nothing. And if I give all my possessions to feed the poor, and if I deliver my body to be burned, but do not have love, it profits me nothing" (1Co. 13:1-3).

Ordained Through Angels by the Agency of a Mediator

"Why the Law then? It was added because of transgressions, having been ordained through angels by the agency of a mediator, until the seed should come to whom the promise had been made. Now a mediator is not for one party only; whereas God is only one. Is the Law then contrary to the promises of God? May it never be! For if a law had been given which was able to impart life, then righteousness would indeed have been based on law. But the Scripture has shut up all men under sin, that the promise by faith in Jesus Christ might be given to those who believe" (Gal. 3:19-22).

The Worship of the Angels

"Therefore let no one act as your judge in regard to food or drink or in respect to a festival or a new moon or a Sabbath day—things which are a mere shadow of what is to come; but the substance belongs to Christ. Let no one keep defrauding you of your prize by delighting in self-abasement and the worship of the angels, taking his stand on visions he has seen, inflated without cause by his fleshly mind, and not holding fast to the head, from whom the entire body, being supplied and held together by the joints and ligaments, grows with a growth which is from God" (Col. 2:16-19).

With His Mighty Angels in Flaming Fire

"We ought always to give thanks to God for you, brethren, as is only fitting, because your faith is greatly enlarged, and the love of each one of you toward one another grows ever greater; therefore, we ourselves speak proudly of you among the churches of God for your perseverance and faith in the midst of all your persecutions and afflictions which you endure. This is a plain indication of God's righteous judgment so that you may be considered worthy of the kingdom of God, for which indeed you are suffering. For after all it is only just for God to repay with affliction those who afflict you, and to give relief to you who are afflicted and to us as well when the Lord Jesus shall be revealed from heaven with His mighty angels in flaming fire, dealing out retribution to those who do not know God and to those who do not obey the gospel of our Lord Jesus. And these will pay the penalty of eternal destruction, away from the presence of the Lord and from the glory of His power, when He comes to be glorified in His saints on that day, and to be marveled at among all who have believed—for our testimony to you was believed. To this end also we pray for you always that our God may count you worthy of your calling, and fulfill every desire for goodness and the work of faith with power; in order that the name of our Lord Jesus may be glorified in you, and you in Him, according to the grace of our God and the Lord Jesus Christ" (2Th. 1:3-12).

Seen by Angels

"I am writing these things to you, hoping to come to you before long; but in case I am delayed, I write so that you may know how one ought to conduct himself in the household of God, which is the church of the living God, the pillar and support of the truth. And by common confession great is the mystery of godliness: He who was revealed in the flesh, Was vindicated in the Spirit, Beheld by angels, Proclaimed among the nations, Believed on in the world, Taken up in glory" (1Ti. 3:14-16).

His Chosen Angels

"Let the elders who rule well be considered worthy of double honor, especially those who work hard at preaching and teaching. For the Scripture says, 'YOU SHALL NOT MUZZLE THE OX WHILE HE IS THRESHING,' and 'The laborer is worthy of his wages.' Do not receive an accusation against an elder except on the basis of two or three witnesses. Those who continue in sin, rebuke in the presence of all, so that the rest also may be fearful of sinning. I solemnly charge you in the presence of God and of Christ Jesus and of His chosen angels, to maintain these principles without bias, doing nothing in a spirit of partiality. Do not lay hands upon anyone too hastily and thus share responsibility for the sins of others; keep yourself free from sin" (1Ti. 5:17-22).

Having Become as Much Better than the Angels

"God, after He spoke long ago to the fathers in the prophets in many portions and in many ways, in these last days has spoken to us in His Son, whom He appointed heir of all things, through whom also He made the world. And He is the radiance of His glory and the exact representation of His nature, and upholds all things by the word of His power. When He had made purification of sins, He sat down at the right hand of the Majesty on high; having become as much better than the angels, as He has inherited a more excellent name than they" (Heb. 1:1-4).

Which of the Angels

"For to which of the angels did He ever say, 'THOU ART MY SON, TODAY I HAVE BEGOTTEN THEE'? And again, 'I WILL BE A FATHER TO HIM AND HE SHALL BE A SON TO ME'? And when He again brings the first-born into the world, He says, 'AND LET ALL THE ANGELS OF GOD WORSHIP HIM.' And of the angels He says, 'WHO MAKES HIS ANGELS WINDS, AND HIS MINISTERS A FLAME OF FIRE.' But of the Son He says, 'THY THRONE, O GOD, IS FOREVER AND EVER, AND THE RIGHTEOUS SCEPTER IS THE SCEPTER OF HIS KINGDOM. THOU HAST LOVED RIGHTEOUSNESS AND HATED LAWLESSNESS; THEREFORE GOD, THY GOD, HATH ANOINTED THEE

WITH THE OIL OF GLADNESS ABOVE THY COMPANIONS.' And, 'THOU, LORD, IN THE BEGINNING DIDST LAY THE FOUNDATION OF THE EARTH, AND THE HEAVENS ARE THE WORKS OF THY HANDS; THEY WILL PERISH, BUT THOU REMAINEST; AND THEY ALL WILL BECOME OLD AS A GARMENT, AND AS A MANTLE THOU WILT ROLL THEM UP; AS A GARMENT THEY WILL ALSO BE CHANGED. BUT THOU ART THE SAME, AND THY YEARS WILL NOT COME TO AN END.' But to which of the angels has He ever said, 'SIT AT MY RIGHT HAND, UNTIL I MAKE THINE ENEMIES A FOOTSTOOL FOR THY FEET'? Are they not all ministering spirits, sent out to render service for the sake of those who will inherit salvation" (Heb. 1:5-14)?

The Word Spoken Through Angels Proved Unalterable

"For this reason we must pay much closer attention to what we have heard, lest we drift away from it. For if the word spoken through angels proved unalterable, and every transgression and disobedience received a just recompense, how shall we escape if we neglect so great a salvation? After it was at the first spoken through the Lord, it was confirmed to us by those who heard, God also bearing witness with them, both by signs and wonders and by various miracles and by gifts of the Holy Spirit according to His own will" (Heb. 2:1-4).

Subject to Angels

"For He did not subject to angels the world to come, concerning which we are speaking. But one has testified somewhere, saying, 'WHAT IS MAN, THAT THOU REMEMBEREST HIM? OR THE SON OF MAN,

THAT THOU ART CONCERNED ABOUT HIM? THOU HAST MADE HIM FOR A LITTLE WHILE LOWER THAN THE ANGELS; THOU HAST CROWNED HIM WITH GLORY AND HONOR, AND HAST APPOINTED HIM OVER THE WORKS OF THY HANDS; THOU HAST PUT ALL THINGS IN SUBJECTION UNDER HIS FEET.' For in subjecting all things to him, He left nothing that is not subject to him. But now we do not yet see all things subjected to him. But we do see Him who has been made for a little while lower than the angels, namely, Jesus, because of the suffering of death crowned with glory and honor, that by the grace of God He might taste death for everyone" (Heb. 2:5-9).

For Assuredly He Does Not Give Help to Angels, but He Gives Help to the Descendant of Abraham.

"Since then the children share in flesh and blood, He Himself likewise also partook of the same, that through death He might render powerless him who had the power of death, that is, the devil; and might deliver those who through fear of death were subject to slavery all their lives. For assuredly He does not give help to angels, but He gives help to the descendant of Abraham. Therefore, He had to be made like His brethren in all things, that He might become a merciful and faithful high priest in things pertaining to God, to make propitiation for the sins of the people. For since He Himself was tempted in that which He has suffered, He is able to come to the aid of those who are tempted" (Heb. 2:14-18).

To Myriads of Angels

"For you have not come to a mountain that may be touched and to a blazing fire, and to darkness and gloom and whirlwind, and to the blast of a trumpet and the sound of words which sound was such that those who heard begged that no further word should be spoken to them. For they could not bear the command, 'IF EVEN A BEAST TOUCHES THE MOUNTAIN, IT WILL BE STONED.' And so terrible was the sight, that Moses said, 'I AM FULL OF FEAR AND TREMBLING.' But you have come to Mount Zion and to the city of the living God, the heavenly Jerusalem, and to myriads of angels, to the general assembly and church of the first-born who are enrolled in heaven, and to God, the Judge of all, and to the spirits of righteous men made perfect, and to Jesus, the mediator of a new covenant, and to the sprinkled blood, which speaks better than the blood of Abel" (Heb. 12:18-24).

Some Have Entertained Angels Without Knowing It

"Let love of the brethren continue. Do not neglect to show hospitality to strangers, for by this some have entertained angels without knowing it. Remember the prisoners, as though in prison with them, and those who are ill-treated, since you yourselves also are in the body. Let marriage be held in honor among all, and let the marriage bed be undefiled; for fornicators and adulterers God will judge. Let your character be free from the love of money, being content with what you have; for He Himself has said, 'I WILL NEVER DESERT YOU, NOR WILL I EVER FORSAKE YOU,' so that we confidently say, 'THE LORD IS MY HELPER, I WILL NOT BE AFRAID. WHAT SHALL MAN DO TO ME'" (Heb. 13:1-6)?

Things into which Angels Long to Look

"As to this salvation, the prophets who prophesied of the grace that would come to you made careful search and inquiry, seeking to know what person or time the Spirit of Christ within them was indicating as He predicted the sufferings of Christ and the glories to follow. It was revealed to them that they were not serving themselves, but you, in these things which now have been announced to you through those who preached the gospel to you by the Holy Spirit sent from heaven — things into which angels long to look" (1Pe. 1:10-12).

Angels, Authorities, Powers Had Been Subjected to Him

"And who is there to harm you if you prove zealous for what is good? But even if you should suffer for the sake of righteousness, you are blessed. AND DO NOT FEAR THEIR INTIMIDATION, AND DO NOT BE TROUBLED, but sanctify Christ as Lord in your hearts, always being ready to make a defense to everyone who asks you to give an account for the hope that is in you, yet with gentleness and reverence; and keep a good conscience so that in the thing in which you are slandered, those who revile your good behavior in Christ may be put to shame. For it is better, if God should will it so, that you suffer for doing what is right rather than for doing what is wrong. For Christ also died for sins once for all, the just for the unjust, in order that He might bring us to God, having been put to death in the flesh, but made alive in the spirit; in which also He went and made proclamation to the spirits now in prison, who once were disobedient, when the patience of God kept waiting in the days of Noah, during the construction of the ark, in which a few, that is, eight persons, were brought safely through the water.

And corresponding to that, baptism now saves you — not the removal of dirt from the flesh, but an appeal to God for a good conscience — through the resurrection of Jesus Christ, who is at the right hand of God, having gone into heaven, after angels and authorities and powers had been subjected to Him" (1Pe. 3:13-22).

God Did Not Spare Angels when They Sinned

"For if God did not spare angels when they sinned, but cast them into hell and committed them to pits of darkness, reserved for judgment; and did not spare the ancient world, but preserved Noah, a preacher of righteousness, with seven others, when He brought a flood upon the world of the ungodly; and if He condemned the cities of Sodom and Gomorrah to destruction by reducing them to ashes, having made them an example to those who would live ungodly thereafter; and if He rescued righteous Lot, oppressed by the sensual conduct of unprincipled men (for by what he saw and heard that righteous man, while living among them, felt his righteous soul tormented day after day with their lawless deeds), then the Lord knows how to rescue the godly from temptation, and to keep the unrighteous under punishment for the day of judgment, and especially those who indulge the flesh in its corrupt desires and despise authority. Daring, self-willed, they do not tremble when they revile angelic majesties, whereas angels who are greater in might and power do not bring a reviling judgment against them before the Lord. But these, like unreasoning animals, born as creatures of instinct to be captured and killed, reviling where they have no knowledge, will in the destruction of those creatures also be destroyed, suffering wrong as the wages of doing wrong. They count it a pleasure to revel in the daytime. They are stains and blemishes, reveling in their deceptions, as they carouse with you, having eyes full of adultery and that never cease from sin, enticing unstable souls, having a heart trained in greed, accursed children; forsaking the right way they have gone astray, having followed the way of Balaam, the son of Beor, who loved the wages of unrighteousness, but he received a rebuke for his own transgression; for a dumb donkey, speaking with a voice of a man, restrained the madness of the prophet" (2Pe. 2:4-16).

Angels Who Did Not Keep Their Own Domain

"Now I desire to remind you, though you know all things once for all, that the Lord, after saving a people out of the land of Egypt, subsequently destroyed those who did not believe. And angels who did not keep their own domain, but abandoned their proper abode, He has kept in eternal bonds under darkness for the judgment of the great day. Just as Sodom and Gomorrah and the cities around them, since they in the same way as these indulged in gross immorality and went after strange flesh, are exhibited as an example, in undergoing the punishment of eternal fire" (Jude 1:5-7).

The Seven Stars Are the Angels of the Seven Churches

"And when I saw Him, I fell at His feet as a dead man. And He laid His right hand upon me, saying, 'Do not be afraid; I am the first and the last, and the living One; and I was dead, and behold, I am alive forevermore, and I have the keys of death and of Hades. Write therefore the things which you have seen, and the things which are, and the things which shall take place after these things. As for the mystery of the seven stars which you saw in My right hand, and the seven golden lampstands: the seven stars are the angels of the seven churches, and the seven lampstands are the seven churches'" (Rev. 1:17-20).

Before My Father and Before His Angels

"And to the angel of the church in Sardis write: He who has the seven Spirits of God, and the seven stars, says this: 'I know your deeds, that you have a name that you are alive, but you are dead. Wake up, and strengthen the things that remain, which were about to die; for I have not found your deeds completed in the sight of My God. Remember therefore what you have received and heard; and keep it, and repent. If therefore you will not wake up, I will come like a thief, and you will not know at what hour I will come upon you. But you have a few people in Sardis who have not soiled their garments; and they will walk with Me in white; for they are worthy. He who overcomes shall thus be clothed in white garments; and I will not erase his name from the book of life, and I will confess his name before My Father, and before His angels. He who has an ear, let him hear what the Spirit says to the churches'" (Rev. 3:1-6).

The Voice of Many Angels Around the Throne

"And I looked, and I heard the voice of many angels around the throne and the living creatures and the elders; and the number of them was myriads of myriads, and thousands of thousands, saying with a loud voice, 'Worthy is the Lamb that was slain to receive power and riches and wisdom and might and honor and glory and blessing.' And every created thing which is in heaven and on the earth and under the earth and on the sea, and all things in them, I heard saying, 'To Him who sits on the throne, and to the Lamb, be blessing and honor and glory and dominion forever and ever.' And the four living creatures kept saying, 'Amen.' And the elders fell down and worshiped" (Rev. 5:11-14).

Four Angels Standing at the Four Corners of the Earth

"After this I saw four angels standing at the four corners of the earth, holding back the four winds of the earth, so that no wind should blow on the earth or on the sea or on any tree. And I saw another angel ascending from the rising of the sun, having the seal of the living God; and he cried out with a loud voice to the four angels to whom it was granted to harm the earth and the sea, saying, 'Do not harm the earth or the sea or the trees, until we have sealed the bond-servants of our God on their foreheads'" (Rev. 7:1-3).

All the Angels Were Standing Around the Throne

"After these things I looked, and behold, a great multitude, which no one could count, from every nation and all tribes and peoples and tongues, standing before the throne and before the Lamb, clothed in white robes, and palm branches were in their hands; and they cry out with a loud voice, saying, 'Salvation to our God who sits on the throne, and to the Lamb.' And all the angels were standing around the throne and around the elders and the four living creatures; and they fell on their faces before the throne and worshiped God, saying, 'Amen, blessing and glory and wisdom and thanksgiving and honor and power and might, be to our God forever and ever. Amen'" (Rev. 7:9-12).

Chapter Five

I Saw Seven Angels

"And when He broke the seventh seal, there was silence in heaven for about half an hour. And I saw the seven angels who stand before God; and seven trumpets were given to them" (Rev. 8:1-2).

The Angels Had Seven Trumpets

"And the seven angels who had the seven trumpets prepared themselves to sound them" (Rev. 8:6).

Three Angels

"And I looked, and I heard an eagle flying in midheaven, saying with a loud voice, 'Woe, woe, woe, to those who dwell on the earth, because of the remaining blasts of the trumpet of the three angels who are about to sound'" (Rev. 8:13)!

Release the Four Angels

"And the sixth angel sounded, and I heard a voice from the four horns of the golden altar which is before God, one saying to the sixth angel who had the trumpet, 'Release the four angels who are bound at the great river Euphrates.' And the four angels, who had been prepared for the hour and day and month and year, were released, so that they might kill a third of mankind. And the number of the armies of the horsemen was two hundred million; I heard the number of them. And this is how I saw in the vision the horses and those who sat on them: the riders had breastplates the color of fire and of hyacinth and of brimstone; and the heads of the horses are like the heads of lions; and out of their mouths proceed fire and smoke and brimstone. A third of mankind was killed by these three plagues, by the fire and the smoke and the brimstone, which proceeded out of their mouths. For the power of the horses is in their mouths and in their tails; for their tails are like serpents and have heads; and with them they do harm" (Rev. 9:13-19).

Michael and His Angels Waging War with the Dragon

"And there was war in heaven, Michael and his angels waging war with the dragon. And the dragon and his angels waged war, and they were not strong enough, and there was no longer a place found for them in heaven. And the great dragon was thrown down, the serpent of old who is called the devil and Satan, who deceives the whole world; he was thrown down to the earth, and his angels were thrown down with him. And I heard a loud voice in heaven, saying, 'Now the salvation, and the power, and the kingdom of our God and the authority of His Christ have come, for the accuser of our brethren has been thrown down, who accuses them before our God day and night. And they overcame him because of the blood of the Lamb and because of the word of their testimony, and they did not love their life even to death. For this reason, rejoice, O heavens and you who dwell in them. Woe to the earth and the sea, because the devil has come down to you, having great wrath, knowing that he has only a short time'" (Rev. 12:7-12).

In the Presence of the Holy Angels

"And another angel, a third one, followed them, saying with a loud voice, 'If anyone worships the beast and his image, and receives a mark on his forehead or upon his hand, he also will drink of the wine of the wrath of God, which is mixed in full strength in the cup of His anger; and he will be tormented with fire and brimstone in the presence of the holy angels and in the presence of the Lamb. And the smoke of their torment goes up forever and ever; and they have no rest day and night, those who worship the beast and his image, and whoever receives the mark of his name.' Here is the perseverance of the saints who keep the commandments of God and their faith in Jesus" (Rev. 14:9-12).

Seven Angels Who Had Seven Plagues

"And I saw another sign in heaven, great and marvelous, seven angels who had seven plagues, which are the last, because in them the wrath of God is finished" (Rev. 15:1).

Gave to the Seven Angels Seven Golden Bowls Full of the Wrath of God

"After these things I looked, and the temple of the tabernacle of testimony in heaven was opened, and the seven angels who had the seven plagues came out of the temple, clothed in linen, clean and bright, and girded around their breasts with golden girdles. And one of the four living creatures gave to the seven angels seven golden bowls full of the wrath of God, who lives forever and ever. And the temple was filled with smoke from the glory of God and from His power; and no one was able to enter the temple until the seven plagues of the seven angels were finished" (Rev. 15:5-8).

Saying to the Seven Angels, Go

"And I heard a loud voice from the temple, saying to the seven angels, 'Go and pour out the seven bowls of the wrath of God into the earth'" (Rev. 16:1).

The Angel Said I Will Show You the Judgment

"And one of the seven angels who had the seven bowls came and spoke with me, saying, 'Come here, I shall show you the judgment of the great harlot who sits on many waters, With whom the kings of the earth committed acts of immorality, and those who dwell on the earth were made drunk with the wine of her immorality.' And he carried me away in the Spirit into a wilderness; and I saw a woman sitting on a scarlet beast, full of blasphemous names, having seven heads and ten horns. And the woman was clothed in purple and scarlet, and adorned with gold and precious stones and pearls, having in her hand a gold cup full of abominations and of the unclean things of her immorality, and upon her forehead a name was written, a mystery, 'BABYLON THE GREAT, THE MOTHER OF HARLOTS AND OF THE ABOMINATIONS OF THE EARTH.' And I saw the woman drunk with the blood of the saints, and with the blood of the witnesses of Jesus. And when I saw her, I wondered greatly. And the angel said to me, 'Why do you wonder? I shall tell you the mystery of the woman and of the beast that carries her, which has the seven heads and the ten horns'" (Rev. 17:1-7).

The Angel Said I Will Show You the Bride

"And one of the seven angels who had the seven bowls full of the seven last plagues, came and spoke with me, saying, 'Come here, I shall show you the bride, the wife of the Lamb.' And he carried me away in the Spirit to a great and high mountain, and showed me the holy city, Jerusalem, coming down out of heaven from God, having the glory of God. Her brilliance was like a very costly stone, as a stone of crystal-clear jasper. It had a great and high wall, with twelve gates, and at the gates twelve angels; and names were written on them, which are those of the twelve tribes of the sons of Israel. There were three gates on the east and three gates on the north and three gates on the south and three gates on the west. And the wall of the city had twelve foundation stones, and on them were the twelve names of the twelve apostles of the Lamb" (Rev. 21:9-14).

DAILY FAITH CONFESSIONS
(These are not direct quotations from the Bible but
are paraphrased confessions based on scripture.)
SAY THEM OUT LOUD.

I am God's child (Jn. 1:12). I am royalty (1 Pet. 2:9). I am hidden with Christ in God (Col. 3:3). I am united with the Lord (1 Cor. 6:17). I am a friend of Christ (Jn. 15:15). I am raised up with Him, and seated with Him in heavenly places in Christ Jesus (Eph. 2:6). I was bought with a price (1 Cor. 6:19-20). I am blessed when I come in, and blessed shall I be when I go out (Deut. 28:6). I am a personal witness of Christ (Acts 1:8). I am a saint who prays in the Holy Spirit to keep myself in the love of God (Jude 1:20-21). I draw near with confidence to the throne of grace (Heb. 4:16). I have been adopted by the Father (Eph. 1:5). I am the salt and light of the earth (Mt. 5:13). I am the head and not the tail, and I am above, and not underneath (Deut. 28:13). I have authority to trample serpents and scorpions and over all the power of the enemy (Lk. 10:19). I am a member of the body of Christ (1 Cor. 12:27). God blessed me to be fruitful, and multiply, and replenish the earth, and subdue it: and have dominion (Gen. 1:28). I cannot be separated from God's love (Ro. 8:39). The good work God has begun in me will be perfected (Phil. 1:5). I can do all things through Christ who strengthens me (Phil. 4:13). No weapon that is formed against me will prosper (Is. 54:17). So then faith cometh by hearing, and hearing by the word of God (Ro. 10:17 KJV). Faith is my currency to operate in the kingdom of God (Ro. 14:23). I am God's workmanship created in Christ Jesus for good works, which God prepared beforehand (Eph. 2:10). I have been appointed to bear fruit, and that my fruit would remain (Jn. 15:16). I am being wise when I am winning souls for King Jesus (Pr. 11:30). My body is the temple of the Holy Spirit (1 Cor. 6:19). I have access to God through the Holy Spirit (Eph. 2:18). I have been justified (Ro. 5:1). Therefore there is now no condemnation for those who are in Christ Jesus (Ro. 8:1). Greater is He who is in me than he who is in the world (1 Jn. 4:4). I will do greater works than Jesus because He went to the Father (Jn. 14:12). As God was with Moses, He will be with me; God will not fail me or forsake me (Jos. 1:5). I see myself the way God see me. God sees me as a king (Gen, 17:6, Rev. 1:6) God sees me as royalty (1 Pet. 2:9). God sees me as the righteousness of God in Christ, bold as a lion (Ro. 3:22, Pr. 28:1). God sees me without spot or wrinkle because of the blood of Jesus (1 Pet. 1:19). I am having faith for big things because God owns everything and I'm His son (Ps. 24:1). No man will be able to stand before me all the days of my life (Jos. 1:5). My Father is glorified by this that I bear much fruit, and proves I'm a disciple (see Jn. 15:8). I think big and confess big things because God is big (Ps. 24:1). I will respect God for the big God that He is and my mouth will create whatever I want (Lk. 6:45). I no longer think of millions, my renewed mind thinks of billions because the wealth of the wicked is laid up for the righteous (Pr. 13:22). The sinner's job is to gather and collect for the one who is good in God's sight (Ecc. 2:26). Redemption is not complete without prosperity. Jesus hung on the cross so I can have the whole package, not just salvation (2 Cor. 8:9). I don't have to qualify, Jesus has qualified me. Jesus reversed the curse. The devil is a liar, and Jesus is the Messiah. Jesus is made unto me wisdom, righteousness, sanctification, and redemption (1 Cor. 1:30). I submit to God, I resist the devil and he flees from me (Jas. 4:7). For God has not given me the spirit of fear; but of power, and of love, and of a sound mind (2 Tim. 1:7). The Holy Spirit will teach me all things (Jn. 14:26). The Holy Spirit will guide me into all truth (Jn.16:13). The Holy Spirit abides in me, and I don't need anyone to teach me, but the anointing teaches me all things (1 Jn. 2:27). I quench fiery darts from the wicked one with the shield of faith (Eph. 6:16). I stand firm against the schemes of the devil (Eph. 6:11). I already have the victory and Satan cannot back me up. I advance and hold. Advance and hold to victory after victory (2 Cor. 2:14). I walk in love and live by faith (Gal. 5:6). I have been redeemed from the curse of the law, poverty, sickness, and spiritual death (Gal. 3:13; Deut. 28). I bear much fruit. I'm God's workmanship created beforehand for good works (Eph. 2:10). God's favor is on my life (Ps. 3:8). God blesses me and His favor surrounds me as with a shield (Ps. 5:12). The kingdom of God is within me (Lk. 17:21). I have a production plant inside of me that bears fruit to change the world (Gen. 1:28). God gives me power to get wealth to establish His covenant on earth (Deut. 8:18). I am blessed to be a blessing (Gen. 12:2). I have Satan on the run and will make a mockery of him (Jas. 4:7). No man will be able to stand before me all the days of my life (Jos. 1:5). Faith works through love and love never fails (Gal. 5:6; 1 Cor. 13:8). Thank you Father!

PRAYER FOR SALVATION

Say the following prayer out loud.

Heavenly Father, I am a sinner and I need a Savior. I confess Jesus Christ as the Lord of my life. I repent of all my sins. Father, I truly believe you raised Jesus from the dead. Father, give me spiritual hunger to spend time in Your Word day and night so my mind is renewed. I understand that by meditating and submitting to Your Word daily I will be transformed into the image of Jesus, day-by-day. Thank you, Father, for Your goodness, mercy, and grace. I pray in Jesus' name. Amen.

PRAYER FOR BAPTISM OF THE HOLY SPIRIT

Father, I am your child because Jesus is my Lord. Jesus said, "How much more shall your heavenly Father give the Holy Spirit to those who ask Him." I ask you now in the name of Jesus to fill me with the Holy Spirit. Thank you, Father, I received the baptism of the Holy Spirit by faith. I yield my vocal organs and expect to speak in tongues as the Holy Spirit gives me utterance in Jesus name. Father, I plan to pray in the Holy Spirit building myself up on my most holy faith, and keep myself in the love of God, as mentioned in Jude 20 and 21. In Jesus name I decree it. Amen.

ABOUT THE AUTHOR

Eugene Carvalho is the founder of Receiving by Faith. He is an administrator and Christian author of seventy books. God uses him in the offices of pastor, evangelist and prophet. He holds a bachelor's degree in biblical studies and a double minor in pastoral ministry and world missions. He also holds a master's degree in practical theology. Eugene prayed for a translator and God sent his wife Mercedes who has a six-year degree in Spanish from a university in Tampico, Mexico. They have participated in evangelism in the streets of Mexico for many years. They have also traveled to churches all over the United States and Mexico winning souls and preaching faith. Their current ministry website is: www.receivingbyfaith.org

BOOKS BY EUGENE IN ENGLISH

To purchase other books by Eugene Carvalho visit receivingbyfaith.org or amazon.com.

Receiving by Faith
Faith for Every Day: 365 Daily Devotions
Faith Cometh by Hearing, and Hearing by the Word of God
Faith, Hope, and Love
Walk in Love and Live by Faith
Topical Christian Handbook and Scripture Guide
The Gospel Is the Power of God unto Salvation
Seed Time and Harvest Time
Your New Identity in Christ
The Cross and the Blood
The Holy Spirit
The Attributes of God
The Favor of God
The Glory of God
The Grace of God
The Power of God
The Promises of God
The Spirit of God
The Throne of God
The New Testament Church: A Survey from the Book of Ephesians
Vengeance and Recompense
God's Angel's
Prayer and Fasting
God's Mighty Prophets
A Survey of Jesus Through the Epistles

The Names of Jesus
Old Testament Miracles
New Testament Miracles
The Psalms of David
Mountain Moving Confessions
Visions and Dreams
Blessed Beyond Measure
The Righteous Will Flourish like The Palm Tree
Christ Heals: What the Bible Has to Say
My Peace I Give to You
Balancing Grace and Truth
Praise and Worship Changes Everything
Understanding the Importance of Authority
If You Are Willing and Obedient
Have Life More Abundantly
Sing Unto the Lord a New Song
The Power of the Tongue
The Supernatural: What the Bible Has to Say
The Truth Will Make You Free
Joy in the Holy Ghost
Praise Is Powerful: What the Bible Has to Say
Stewardship Regarding Our Finances
Love, Joy, and Peace Are Fruit of the Holy Ghost
Oh, Give Thanks to the Lord for He Is Good
The Kingdom of Heaven is at Hand
Acquiring Wisdom Is Vital
Grace and Mercy: What the Bible Has to Say
God Is Faithful: What the Bible Has to Say
God Is Love: What the Bible Has to Say
The God of Hope: What the Bible Has to Say
Pearls of Wisdom and Gems of Knowledge
Regarding Christianity

BOOKS BY EUGENE IN SPANISH

Las Promesas de Dios
Los Salmos de David
Lo Sobrenatural: Lo que la Bíblia Tiene que
Decir
Una Mirada Topica Del Libro De Los Salmos
Dios es Amor: Lo que la Biblia Tiene que Decir
La Adquisición de la Sabiduría es Vital: Lo que
la Biblia Tiene que Decir

NOTES

NOTES

NOTES

www.ingramcontent.com/pod-product-compliance
Lightning Source LLC
Chambersburg PA
CBHW070811240726
48654CB00007B/304